WHERE HAVE ALL OUR VALUES GONE?

WHERE HAVE ALL OUR VALUES GONE?

The Decline of Values in America and What We Can Do About It

Andrew Schoedinger, Ph.D.

Copyright © 2004 by Andrew Schoedinger.

ISBN :   Softcover   1-4134-5411-9

All rights reserved. No part of this book may be reproduced or transmitted in any form or by any means, electronic or mechanical, including photocopying, recording, or by any information storage and retrieval system, without permission in writing from the copyright owner.

This book was printed in the United States of America.

To order additional copies of this book, contact:
Xlibris Corporation
1-888-795-4274
www.Xlibris.com
Orders@Xlibris.com
23783

CONTENTS

INTRODUCTION 7

PART I

CHAPTER ONE
   John Dewey and Progressive Education 15
CHAPTER TWO
   Dr. Benjamin Spock and Enlightened Child Care 23
CHAPTER THREE
   Ethical Relativism 32
CHAPTER FOUR
   The Fifties 39
CHAPTER FIVE
   Student Rebellion and the Counterculture 48
CHAPTER SIX
   Vietnam 59
CHAPTER SEVEN
   The Corruption of the Legal System 67
CHAPTER EIGHT
   Television, Music and Hollywood 75
CHAPTER NINE
   The Age of Narcissism 83

PART II

CHAPTER TEN
   Man, The Moral Creature 93
CHAPTER ELEVEN
   Duty 97
CHAPTER TWELVE
   Evil 106

CHAPTER THIRTEEN
  Virtue 111
CHAPTER FOURTEEN
  Authenticity, Self-Esteem and Happiness 119

BIBLIOGRAPHY 125

INTRODUCTION

The writing of this book was motivated by concerns we all seem to share about American society and the apparent disappearance of what has come to be known as "family values." We can hardly get through a day without hearing or reading about family values in one context or another. Politicians, religious leaders and educators all seem to be concerned with this subject yet they never seem to have a reasonable definition of "family values."

The constituents of these leaders, the grass roots of our society, feel a similar concern about family values. When the question is asked of them, however, "What are family values?" no one seems to have an answer that makes sense. Nevertheless, these concerned people share a certain frustration, a feeling that "things" are not as they should be in America. They also seem to share the sense that if we could just return to the family values of an earlier time, things would once again be all right. Yet few people, if any, that I know or know of, are anti-family or against the values that traditional families embody. Surveys taken conclude that most people enthusiastically support marriage and raising families, they generally seem to disapprove of adultery, and they want their kids to grow up to be law-abiding members of society. Along with the underlying frustration, there seems to be a bit of nostalgia. People seem to want to return to:

> A past time that was more tranquil and stable.
> A time when drugs and crime were not rampant.
> A time when parents didn't have to worry about their children's safety at school.
> A time when providers of entertainment were not obsessed with gratuitous sex and violence.

> A time when people were civil and good manners were typical.
> A time when kids could play unattended by an adult without fear of being abducted or molested in some way.

So, precisely what is it that people mean by family values? I submit that we have adopted this phrase to describe moral and social well-being. I believe, our country has a crisis of moral and social well-being on its hands. We seem to be entering the 21st century in a state of moral and social decline. People sense this and are concerned. Some talk show hosts submit that we are facing this problem because we no longer spank our children. Other concerned people say institutions have taken our rights as parents away. Still others blame the decay on video games, comic books, and other media. But what all of America seems to share is frustration because we don't know what precisely to do about it. People feel helpless about what they can do to turn things around to put a halt to the moral and social decline. That an overwhelming number of people feel this way is understandable. I submit that we cannot find a solution to this moral decline and halt the vanishing of our values unless we first understand the complexity of causes that have brought us to where we are today. Only then can a coherent solution to the problem be developed and carried out. This book seeks to do both; to review the causes and recommend solutions.

Although it may appear that the causes for the decline of values in our society are isolated and independent, they are the result of many contributing factors. These are interconnected much as are the overlapping fibers in a length of rope. Once we come to understand how we got ourselves in the mess that we are in, we can begin to construct a way out of it. The good news is that we, as human beings, have the power to right the moral and social course of this country. But to reverse our moral decline will require widespread personal commitment on the part of the American people.

Such a commitment, first and foremost, requires individuals to take full responsibility for their behavior. We all make mistakes. When we do, we must refrain from pointing a finger at someone else. We must own up to our mistakes and willingly pay the price.

Furthermore, people must give up the all-too-pervasive victim mentality, the mindset that "I am not at fault because I suffer from some physical or psychological handicap." And people need to stop blaming society at large for all their ills. Ultimately, what all this means is that people must take back control of their own lives and understand that they own their behavior and are therefore responsible for it. As the saying goes, "The buck stops here." And here means each one of us. Without such a personal commitment, the future of this country is highly questionable.

Moral values vs. "culture wars"

Practically everyone in this society will agree that we have experienced over the past several decades a crisis of values. To appreciate this book's analysis, it is necessary to establish the distinction between the decline in the moral and social values within our society and the "culture wars" also raging within it. The battles over the right to an abortion versus the right to life, the conflict over capital punishment, the hostility surrounding disputed rights of homosexuals and controversy over physician-assisted suicide are examples of the culture wars that presently are taking place.

These culture wars are different than the decline in moral and social values in that culture wars have their roots in religious doctrine. Take religion out of the mix and these conflicts would dwindle. The present culture wars are relatively recent and even though some would argue that it is the decline in religion that has been the main factor in the destruction of family values, the demographics of religion do not substantiate such a claim. Whereas such demographics have shifted over the course of the 20th century, it nevertheless remains the case that Americans, by and large, are adherents of some religious persuasion or other. Religion and the values it promotes are not in decline. That there is no universal consensus concerning these religious values is at the core of our culture wars. Two very devout religious people can be on opposite sides of the fence concerning abortion, capital punishment, euthanasia and homosexuality.

There is a tendency on the part of some people to think that all of our troubles are the result of a decline in **moral** values. This contributes to the confusion between the decline in values and our culture wars. This tendency exists because all religions advocate a moral code; for example, the moral codes of Judaism and Christianity are rooted in the Ten Commandments as found in The Bible. There is no doubt that there has been a decline in moral values over the course of the 20th century. That, however, is only one aspect of the crisis of values we are experiencing. Many of the values that have declined have nothing whatsoever to do with morality. Patriotism, for example, is a value that exists independently of a moral code. As **Chapters One through Nine** demonstrate, non-moral values play an integral role in our present values crisis. Yet, these non-moral values play absolutely no role in our culture wars.

The values that define our present culture wars are moral values. These culture wars are disputes over moral values. Typically, the side of the fence one is on in such quarrels is dictated by the religious viewpoint one takes with respect to issues being disputed. A difference of opinion over the morality of physician-assisted suicide is a dispute between the presumed right of self-determination and the sanctity of life. Culture wars, as with every other kind of war, are battles between two viable sides.

The decline in values throughout the course of the 20th century has not been the result of a culture war. Such a decline has developed in an evolutionary way with values being chipped away a little at a time. The concern over the decline of any one of the values discussed in **Chapters One through Nine** has been after the fact of that decline, not as a defining feature of the decline itself. This book is not about culture wars but rather is an analysis of the decline of both moral and non-moral values over the course of the 20th century.

Religious And Other Authority

We do not develop our values in a vacuum. They come to us from some authority with God being the ultimate authority. But just what is authority? It is a power to influence thoughts and opinions and the outward behaviors of individuals. Such influence is either mental or physical or both. All authority dictates some value or set of values. There is no authority that can successfully dictate, however, unless it has the power to enforce those dictates. Influence and enforcement, either real or imagined go hand-in-hand. Genuine authority gives clout to values.

There are many sources of authority. Aside from God, there is the authority of parents, educators, and government. When a source of authority is called into question, the values that authority dictates are challenged and to some extent undermined. The decline of values in 20th century America has a great deal to do with the challenges presented over the last hundred years to the traditional sources of authority in our country.

There is a price to be paid when authority is undermined. If it is not adequately replaced, people typically assume that they are accountable to no one or no institution. Such lack of accountability undermines freedom. It sets the stage for anarchy, a state in which there are no rules governing behavior and, therefore, anything goes. In addition, it leads to normally law-abiding citizens feeling threatened by the lack of certainty in their everyday lives. What they have always relied upon as being safe no longer feels that way to them.

If one source of authority is not replaced by another traditional one, the only option is to place oneself in that position of authority. To assume authority, as an individual, requires a great deal of self-discipline because it entails allowing reason to rule our passions. It entails a commitment to doing what we ought to do even though at the time we would really rather not. If, however, we can regulate ourselves and take personal responsibility for our actions, we can arrive at a better society for all of us. Such self-regulation can only be successful if it is guided by a set of values. So where do those values come from if not from some source of authority outside of ourselves? We, as the rational creatures we are, have the ability to figure out what is of value and what principles we ought let guide our behavior. These values and principles function as laws of behavior and are the basis of freedom. By adhering to such laws of behavior, we become responsible moral and social individuals. **Chapters Eleven, Twelve and Thirteen** demonstrate that these laws of behavior are the same for everyone and that ethical relativism is a flawed doctrine and must be rejected.

Where do we go from here?

Chapters One though Nine analyze the causes of the decline of values. We often have a tendency to look for one underlying cause of this decline but if we think about it, hardly anything in life is the result of just one factor. The decline of values in our society is no exception. There has not been one cause of this phenomenon. Rather, it has been a series of events resulting from an interpretation and/or misinterpretation of ideas by thinkers during the last hundred years. Granted, it would be much easier to boil everything down to one specific cause but that can't be done in this situation.

Chapters Ten, Eleven and Twelve deal specifically with morality and moral values. Man is uniquely a moral creature and, therefore, has what it takes to be a source of moral authority if he so chooses.

Chapter Thirteen is an analysis of virtue and virtuous behavior. Some virtues are rooted in morality and some are not. Virtues, of course, play an integral role in any comprehensive discussion of values.

Chapter Fourteen deals with quality of life issues. All people pretty much want to be happy but wanting it is certainly no guarantee that we will attain such status. Happiness, like anything else of value, may be difficult to attain but assuredly there is no genuine quality of life without happiness. Values are essential to happiness.

PART I

CHAPTER ONE

John Dewey and Progressive Education

Values Under Attack: Self-Discipline and Perseverance

At the very beginning of the 20th century, the garden path leading to our moral decline as a nation began with the theory proposed by American philosopher John Dewey, the leader of the progressive education movement. Throughout this century, progressive education has transformed primary and secondary education. In the process, the values of self-discipline and perseverance have been compromised. The attack upon these values was inevitable due to the utopian nature of the progressive education theory. Like many a theory, this one looks good on paper but simply doesn't work. A little background helps explain what led Dewey to formulate his radical ideas.

At the turn of the century barely one percent of America's entire school population went to college and only five percent acquired a high school diploma. Far more than half the students left on or before completion of the fifth year of elementary school. Prior to the Industrial Revolution, practical education, that which one needed to eke out a living, took place on the family farm. The Industrial Revolution, however, replaced the traditional rural-based economy of this country with an urban one as people migrated from farms to centers of industry turning towns into cities. Dewey saw the need for vocational education since most students were destined to join the labor force in the industries that drove the new economy. Dewey's educational reforms were targeted to this segment of society.

John Dewey believed that the vast majority of students who drop out of school at an early age do so because it is boring. Traditional education is based on the memorization of facts with skills being developed by rote and listening. A listening-based curriculum provides uniformity of material and method which makes for efficiency in the teaching process. According to Dewey, however, the listening model carries with it three disadvantages. In the first place, it makes the subject matter purely formal and symbolic and, consequently, sterile and impersonal. Second, the lack of relevance of subject matter to the lives of students undermines any motivation for the student to learn. Third, a uniform curriculum presents subject matter in a "canned" format whereby the thought-provoking character of it is obscured. This robs the student of the opportunity to utilize his reasoning powers. In short, the listening model of learning places the student in a passive role with respect to how he learns the prescribed subject matter. When a student is rendered passive, the material presented to him to learn becomes irrelevant and meaningless.

No wonder students were bored stiff! The listening model works for only a small percentage of students. Professor Dewey was convinced there was a way to make the schooling experience meaningful to all students. All children are eager to learn but the ways in which the material is presented to children makes all the difference in their receptivity to that subject matter. What and how much a student learns is completely dependent upon the process by which he learns it. Dewey thought children learned more effectively by being active participants in the learning process. Children are naturally active. From the beginning of their lives they cope with and try to control their environment. To do this successfully they must solve problems. Understandably, solving the problems of their world is what is of interest to them. So it follows that the most effective way for a child to learn a given subject matter is for it to be presented to him within the context of the problems of his world. The role of the instructor is to direct studies as instruments for solving the problems that are of interest *to the students*. For all but a select few, mathematics has no intrinsic value. For the majority, its value lies in being a tool that can be used to solve problems. A child cannot know how many marbles he has to play with unless he knows how to count. The issue here is not learning to count. The issue is knowing precisely how many marbles one has. Dewey thought the student would most effectively learn how to count when he realized how important it is *to him* how to count.

Dewey believed that an effective learning environment involves more than the mere teaching style of an instructor; that is, it involves an entire environment in which the teaching/learning process occurs. A classroom with study desks positioned neatly in rows where students do not speak unless spoken to, where subject matter is rigidly scheduled, a classroom that manifests orderliness in all ways, is a sterile learning environment. If we want to maximize the learning experience, the classroom must be a center of activity. Dewey thought that effective learning occurs within a somewhat chaotic setting. He compares it to a busy workshop. ". . . there is a certain disorder in any busy workshop; there is not silence, persons are not engaged in maintaining certain fixed physical postures; their arms are not folded; they are not holding their books thus and so. They are doing a variety of things, and there is the confusion, the bustle, that results from activity." (*The School and Society,* p. 14.) For example, learning about Native Americans can involve the growing of corn for food and the tanning of hides for clothing. Students would engage in mock fur trading thus learning about the economics of bartering. They would learn the art of building a canoe and in the process determine what sorts of trees work best. They would come to understand the social organization of a tribe through role-playing. The most important factor in the learning process is discovering first-hand what it was to be a Native American before the arrival of the white man by re-creating Native American life experiences as much as possible. This is "learning by doing." From the standpoint of progressive education, reading material on the subject being studied is strictly supplemental.

Not surprisingly, Dewey wanted to see if his theory worked. In 1896 he and his wife established the Laboratory School, so named to emphasize its experimental character. It proved successful. As word of this success spread, educators in general took note. Although Dewey's educational reforms were targeted to a specific segment of the society, his philosophy of education struck a chord nationwide, generating change in both public and private schools from the elementary level through high school. Universities jumped on the bandwagon by developing separate colleges of education devoted primarily to teaching pedagogy, the methods of teaching.

In 1919 the Progressive Education Association was founded. It issued a statement of seven principles:

1) Freedom to Develop Naturally,
2) Interest the Motive of All Work,
3) The Teacher as Guide, Not Task-Master,
4) Scientific Study of Pupil Development,
5) Greater Attention to All that Affects the Child's Physical Development,
6) Co-operation Between School and Home to Meet the Needs of Child-Life and
7) The Progressive School a Leader in Educational Movements.

The intent of the Association was to redesign the entire school system of America and they were successful. During the 1920s and 1930s there was vast educational reform with literally thousands of local school districts adopting various elements in the progressive program. In October 1938, *Time* magazine ran a cover story on the Association, contending: "No U.S. school has completely escaped its influence."

So what is wrong with progressive education? Its fault lies in its utopian nature. The major problem lies in finding enough committed competent teachers to progressively lead the nation's schools. First of all, the commitment on behalf of such teachers must be all-consuming. An examination of the lives of those who taught in successful programs reveals that the program was their life. Second, such teachers must possess an extraordinarily wide range of knowledge to meet the challenge of "integrated studies." Third, they need to be wizards of pedagogical ingenuity. The innovations of progressive education worked wonders when first-rate instructors were in control. Unfortunately, the vast majority of teachers simply did not have the skills or the level of commitment for the movement to be successful. In fact, chaos was the result.

In the 1940s a backlash to the progressive education movement occurred that culminated in 1957 when the Soviet Union beat the United States in the space race by successfully testing an intercontinental ballistic missile (ICBM) and by launching *Sputnik*, a satellite. This prompted a thoroughgoing examination of our schools. Progressive education was deemed to be the culprit in our loss of technological superiority. The condemnation of progressive education was not enough to extinguish it because the majority of the critics were not members of the teaching profession. There has never been a shortage of proponents of Dewey's philosophy of education because teachers have never been able to escape progressive education indoctrination in their quest for a teaching certificate.

Early in the century, various colleges and universities became enthralled with progressive education programs, the content of which was pedagogy. Many of these teacher education programs have developed into full-blown colleges of education within the university. These programs owe their existence to the progressive education movement. When the major emphasis of a program is pedagogy, training in areas of content inevitably gets shortchanged. Consequently, upon receiving a teaching certificate an individual typically is armed with a thorough understanding of *how* to teach but with little expertise in *what* to teach. In essence, the success of the progressive education movement at one level, namely the development of teacher education programs at colleges and universities has sown the seeds of its own destruction at another level, namely the K-12 classroom. Methodology has superceded content, the result being that K-12 students are the beneficiaries of pedagogy but are robbed of a substantive education that includes but is not limited to the acquisition of basic skills in reading, writing, and calculating.

That schools are still feeling the effects of Dewey's philosophy of education is manifested by what became known as "new math" and now "new-new math" verified by an article written by Edward Walsh of The Washington Post.

> CHICAGO—In the beginning there was math. Then, fueled by Sputnik and fear of national disgrace, 'new math' appeared with its focus on theories, which were roundly despised and ultimately discarded. After first retreating to the basic skills of old math, many educators have since come to embrace a curriculum of creative, hands-on exercises that have great appeal to young children. Instead of rote memorization of math facts, students are encouraged to estimate answers or to use calculators. It's come to be known as 'new-new math.' Critics who have railed against math reforms over the past decade call it less charitable names: 'fuzzy math,' 'math lite,' and, in some circles, 'fuzzy crap.' . . . Amidst these raging math wars the nation's largest math teachers association came to Chicago . . . and heartily endorsed a new set of mathematics standards for the next decade and embraced new-new math . . . . In part as a concession to critics, the standards include a strong dose of old math, a reminder that students are expected to learn the basic skills of addition, subtraction, multiplication and division . . . . The new-new math programs encourage students to discover multiple ways to figure out the problems, rather than a single method. For instance, 3rd graders may learn four ways to multiply, and they choose the one that suits them. 'In the drill and kill days, there were set ways to do things,' said Gloria Oggero, a former 8th grade teacher who now works for the regional office of education in

Belleville, Ill. "The kids could do it and get the right answer, but they didn't understand the "why" of it.' . . . Third grade: 'Construct two-dimensional figures out of straws. Compare and contrast two-dimensional figures. Name polygons; triangle, square, rhombus, rectangle, parallelogram and trapezoid. Draw a square or rectangle with a given perimeter.' David Klein, professor of mathematics at the California State University at Northridge, opposes these methods. He complains that the programs too often touch lightly on a number of concepts, failing to delve deeply into any subject. 'It's a sort of scrambled-eggs version of math, like the holistic approach to everything,' Klein said. Supporters say the math programs appeal to all students, rather than a geeky few, and they say critics have not given the new initiatives enough time to prove their worth. Many students, they argue, lose interest in traditional math by junior high school because they find it boring, rigid and not applicable to daily life. The new math programs encourage them to take risks and not be afraid of numbers.[1]

Such progressive approaches to education have contributed greatly to the decline of basic skills nationwide since World War II. Instructors with little background in the subjects they are to teach not surprisingly produce an enormous number of individuals with little or no skills or knowledge. The classroom inescapably turns into an indoor playground, a place where classmates play at learning. This is the inevitable result of pedagogy without substantive direction. It fits nicely the principle, The Teacher a Guide, Not a Task Master. Without some expertise in what to teach, such an individual could not be a task master even if he wanted to because he himself has not mastered any area of substantive concern.

This all nets out to the classroom degenerating into somewhat of a zoo, the hallmark of which is a lack of discipline. This lack of

---

[1] *The Idaho Statesman*, April 13, 2000.

discipline manifests itself in two related ways: a) lack of respect for the teacher and b) failure to master prescribed subject matter. In essence, an inadequate progressive education movement has successfully undermined the authority of the schools. Absent a Laboratory School, students generally need taskmasters for them to develop basic skills. One of the fundamental misconceptions permeating (especially the elementary) schools as a result of the progressive education movement is that *all* learning is fun. It is not all fun. Learning foundations is often a grind. Yet it is in mastering the grind that one learns the value of self-discipline and perseverance.

There is nothing in the progressive education movement that emphasizes the values of self-discipline and perseverance because it is assumed at the outset that if the learning environment is made fun, success in learning is easily had. This view is not only wrong, it is misleading. Without self-discipline and perseverance, failure looms ever present on one's horizon *regardless of one's abilities and goals*. Without authority, the school has no leverage to force students to learn basic skills. Without these basic skills, a student cannot progress either academically or intellectually. Without such development one's self-esteem is inevitably diminished. Without self-esteem, one cannot be happy. An unhappy person is a dissatisfied person; one who is adrift in the sea of life, of little use to himself much less to society.

Without intending it the progressive education movement has contributed to a society wherein individuals expect immediate gratification. Yet success in most endeavors requires perseverance. The expectation of immediate gratification is a fundamental element of narcissism which is discussed in **Chapter Nine**. In order to recapture the values of self-discipline and perseverance, people must come to realize that

> Success is a function of consistency.
> Consistency is a function of practice.
> And practice is a function of self-discipline.

CHAPTER TWO

Dr. Benjamin Spock and Enlightened Child Care

Values Under Attack: Discipline and Responsibility

Published in 1946, Benjamin Spock's *The Common Sense Book of Baby and Child Care*, revolutionized the way in which children in America were raised. His book reflected Dr. Spock's disagreement with existing books on the subject available to those new to the experience of having, caring for, and raising children. They were of the Victorian Age, rigid and devoid of any understanding or appreciation of the child *as a person* in his development. In short, no attention was given to the role of psychology in raising children.

Very early in his career Dr. Spock began to take a holistic approach to medicine; that is that physical ailments can have mental causes. At an intuitive level, he felt that treating only a patient's physical symptoms very often missed understanding the causes of them. During a one-year internship (1931-32) in pediatrics, he decided to take a year's residency in psychiatry. His failure as an analyst early on contributed greatly to his decision to remain in pediatrics but did not lessen his interest in psychology. As an alternative to child psychiatry, Dr. Spock committed himself to "figuring out the application of psychiatric and psychological principles, in a preventive way, within the practice of ordinary pediatrics." Until then that field had not been seriously explored.

As part of his psychoanalytic training subsequent to his psychiatry residency, Dr. Spock attended two seminars a week for the better part of five years. "Here," says he, "I was learning, among other matters, about Freud's concepts of emotional development in children, the phases in their attachment to parents and in their rivalry with parents, the effects of the excessive repression of hostility and sexuality. I was particularly interested, as a pediatrician, in the significance attached to breast feeding, thumb-sucking, toilet training, children's fears."

In 1938, Dr. Spock coauthored an article with Dr. Mabel Huschka "The Psychological Aspects of Pediatric Practice" in which Freudian theory was applied to feeding, weaning, toilet training, discipline and various behavior problems and nervous symptoms. The recommendations of this 50-page landmark went completely counter to the conventional wisdom as expressed in Dr. Luther Holt's *The Care and Feeding of Children: A Catechism for the Use of Mothers and Children's Nurses*. Originally published in 1894, this book set the standard for child rearing for 40 years. It is instructive to note Holt's view on toilet training. He asks, *"How may a child be trained in the action of bowels?* By endeavoring to have them move at exactly the same time every day. *At what age may an infant be trained in this way?* Usually by the second month if training is begun early. *What is the best method of training?* A small chamber, about the size of a pint bowl, is placed between the nurse's knees, and upon this the infant is held, its back against the nurse's chest and its body firmly supported. This should be done twice a day, after the morning and afternoon feedings, and always at the same hour. At first there may be necessary some local irritation, like that produced by tickling the anus or introducing just inside the rectum a small cone of oiled paper or piece of soap, as a suggestion of the purpose for which the baby is placed upon the chamber, but in a surprisingly short time the position is all that is required. With most infants after a few weeks the bowels will move as soon as the infant is placed on the chamber."

In response to this strict approach Drs. Spock and Huschka suggested that "few children can stand the constant interference with their wishes, the steady domination, and remain psychically healthy. They either surrender their spirits and become submissive, or they rebel . . . (The child's) rebelliousness is usually a slow smoldering that brings him no gain, but impairs his own character. The inadmissible hatred arouses anxiety, he turns the resentment against himself and finds ways to hurt himself in the real world or in neurotic symptoms." Consequently, Dr. Spock recommended that the child indicate his own readiness for toilet training, a conclusion reinforced eight years later in his book *Baby and Child Care*. "**Is early bowel training harmful?** . . . Some psychologists think that early training is harmful, in certain cases at least, whether the baby rebels later or not. It seems sensible to give the baby the benefit of the doubt, and leave him in peace until he is old enough to know a little of what it's all about. I would wait until he can at least sit up steadily alone, which will be around 7-9 months . . . . Whether you start bowel training early or late, the most important thing is how you go about it during the *second* year. **Why babies often rebel in the second year.** If a mother is demanding in her training efforts, she goes right against her baby's grain at this age. If she insists that he move his bowels in a certain place at a certain time, she is saying to him in so many words, 'It's not your movement, it's mine. You do it in the place that I choose, when I tell you to.' Instead of appreciating the thing he is proud of, she may show him that she dislikes it. She empties the potty or flushes the toilet as fast as she can, maybe with a look of disgust; It is no wonder that the baby, who's at a balky age anyway, is apt to rebel." (pp. 193-94)

Although Dr. Spock was initially interested in early pediatric care, his book, *Baby and Child Care* is complete. It analyzes child development consistent with Freudian theory through puberty. Dr. Spock thought it best for parents to be aware of and sensitive, if not sympathetic, to the trials and tribulations facing a child as the child progresses through the oral, anal, phallic, latency and puberty stages of development on the road to adulthood.

While attending the above-mentioned seminars, Dr. Spock met Caroline Zachary, a fellow student. Trained in psychoanalysis with elementary school teaching experience, she had earned a Ph.D. in educational psychology under William Kilpatrick. As a graduate student at Columbia University, Kilpatrick had been a star pupil of John Dewey. More than any other, Kilpatrick has been considered the great interpreter and popularizer of Dewey's philosophy of education. Dr. Spock became one of Caroline Zachary's disciples. He says, "From Caroline and other educators I was gaining entirely new ideas about how children learn. Francis Parker, John Dewey, and Kilpatrick had recognized the importance of giving children opportunities to experiment and experience and feel as well as just to learn by rote, enlisting their interest and participation through real life projects appropriate to their age, using each child's strong points to arouse his enthusiasm and thus to overcome his weak points, seeking the reasons when any student was doing poorly in school, keeping in mind the crucial influence of the teacher-pupil relationship in all learning."

So *Baby and Child Care* turned out to be a curious mixture of Freudian psychodynamics and progressive education. It had immediate appeal. Having suffered through the Great Depression followed by a world war, people were ready for a positive outlook on life. Dr. Spock was there telling them to relax, have fun and to enjoy their baby. With his homespun style of writing he humanized the process of raising a child whereas his predecessors had made the process seem artificial, statistical and clinical. He also showed faith in the common sense of parents. At the outset of his book he says, "Trust yourself. You know more than you think you do.... Don't be afraid to trust your own common sense." Within three years of publication, sales of the book had reached a million copies a year. That was only the beginning and with revisions in 1957 and 1968, sales continued to grow. Consequently, Dr. Benjamin Spock had an enormous effect on several generations of American children, especially Baby Boomers and their offspring.

There is no doubt whatsoever that in one sense Dr. Spock espoused permissiveness in raising a child. Tolerance and love are his overriding message. There is a cause for the child's behavior at every stage of development and reason dictates that his development ought not be stifled. This should not be construed, however, as recommending that the parent not offer guidance to the child and to set limits for what is permissible behavior. If parents "naturally lean toward strictness (they) should stick to their guns and raise their children that way." On the other hand, "Parents who incline to an easygoing kind of management... can also raise children who are considerate and cooperative, as long as the parents are not afraid to be firm about those matters that do seem important to them."

Arguably, the book comes up decidedly short on advice about **discipline** and punishment especially at the early stages of child rearing. This is undoubtedly due, in part, to Dr. Spock's negative reaction to the rigidity and often unreasonable methods of Victorian discipline and punishment. It also reflects the influence Freudian theory had on him. A well-adjusted person is one who is not repressed. Victorian discipline which includes corporal punishment is most definitely repressive. Dr. Spock understands corporal punishment to be counterproductive and ill-advised and the attitude of spare the rod and spoil the child is simply a reflection of an unenlightened age. "When (a child) occasionally goes wrong in his early years, he is best straightened out by such methods as distracting, guiding, or even removing him bodily. As he grows older, his parents at times have to explain firmly why he must do this, not do that. If they are sure in their own minds how they expect him to behave, and tell him reasonably, not too irritably, they will have all the control over him that they need." (p. 270)

Suppose, for example, that a toddler demonstrates an interest in a light socket. Rather than a stern 'No' with a slap on the child's hand while he is exploring the socket, "go over promptly and whisk him to another part of the room. Quickly give him a magazine, an empty cigarette box, anything that is safe and interesting." (p.211) The presumption is that the child eventually will understand that light sockets are to be avoided. This is a gratuitous assumption indeed. Time has demonstrated that such permissive means of child rearing sets no understandable limits on the child's behavior and not a bona fide alternative training method. Training entails getting the child to understand what the limits are. This often requires negative reinforcement of a physical nature. Spanking is not necessarily physical abuse. Nor does it warp a child psychologically. Used in moderation it is a most effective training device at the early stage of child development.

Dr. Spock advises that as the child grows older parents should reason with their child when he has committed some transgression. The problem with that, of course, is that reasoning only works as long as the parent and child are working off the same page. Without prior conditioning (training), the child has only his desires as a frame of reference and these are often incompatible with what the parent deems acceptable. Consequently, there is literally no basis for constructive communication.

At a certain age, children need to learn to take **responsibility** for their own behavior. Dr. Spock believes that this comes naturally as a function of family and peer group assimilation. Behavioral characteristics such as stealing between the ages of six and eleven are manifestations of the child's not having a sufficiently warm relationship with his parents or of his feeling inadequate at making friends. Consequently, Dr. Spock opines that to shame the child upon being caught for stealing simply results in him feeling even more isolated. He says, "I don't mean that the parents shouldn't mention the stealing. It's better to get it out in the open in an understanding way. Naturally, the child should return what he has taken, on the basis that the owner will need it. It might be wise for the parent to help make up the sum to be returned, or even to make a present to the child of an object similar to the one he has stolen and returned. This is not a reward for stealing, but a sign that the parent is concerned that the child should not take what isn't his, and that he should have his heart's desire if it is reasonable." (p. 325)

The half century since the original publication of *Baby and Child Care* has demonstrated that such a permissive way of dealing with aberrant behavior constitutes a dereliction of parental duty because it has failed to teach children that they are responsible for their own behavior. Without sanctions imposed by the parents the child does not develop good reasons to accept such responsibility.

Parents (supposedly) having raised a well-adjusted preschooler by being sensitive to Freudian stages of development, have prepared the child to go off to school. At this point, Dewey's influence on Dr. Spock becomes unmistakable. Sections of *Baby and Child Care* reflect the ideas contained in Dewey's *Democracy and Education* and *The School and Society*. In the chapter "What A School Is For," Dr. Spock asserts that, "One job of a school is to make subjects so interesting and real that children will want to learn and remember.... You can only go so far with books and talk. You learn better from actually living the things you are studying. Children will pick up more arithmetic in a week from running a school store, making change, and keeping the books than they will learn in a month out of a book of cold figures. (p. 326) . . . If you start with a topic that is real and interesting, you can use it to teach all manner of subjects. Take the case of a third-grade class in which the work of the year centers around Indians. The more the children find out about Indians the more they want to know. The reader is a story of the Indians, and they really want to know what it says. For arithmetic they study how the Indians counted and what they used for money. Then arithmetic isn't a separate subject at all but a useful part of life. Geography isn't spots on a map. It's where the Indians lived and traveled, and how life on the plains is different from forest life. In science study the children make dyes from berries and dye cloth, or grow corn. They can make bows and arrows and Indian costumes. (p. 327) . . . . A school wants its pupils to learn firsthand about the outside world, about the jobs of the local farmers and businessmen and workers, so that they will see the connection between their schoolwork and real life. It arranges trips to near-by industries, asks people from the outside to come in and talk, encourages classroom discussion. A class that is studying food may have an opportunity, for example, to observe some of the steps in the collecting, pasteurizing, bottling, and delivery of milk, or in the transportation and marketing of vegetables." (p. 329)

Where did Dr. Spock go wrong? We must remember that he

was raised in the ways of the old school, the Victorian approach. He formulated his views with the presupposition that tight parental control was ever present. His recommendation to parents after World War II to "relax" and "trust yourself" was interpreted far more loosely than he had intended. This produced a permissiveness that surprised Dr. Spock and appalled such prominent people as Dr. Norman Vincent Peale, minister and author of *The Power of Positive Thinking*. From his pulpit Dr. Peale castigated Dr. Spock's permissive child-rearing program as "Feed 'em whenever they want, never let them cry, satisfy their every desire." He accused Spock of being responsible for "the most undisciplined age in history." To a great extent, Dr. Peale was correct in his assessment. Instead of well-adjusted, disciplined, eager to learn, cooperative children ready to step out into the world of school, society got unruly, undisciplined, disrespectful, self-centered brats. Although unintended, the effect Dr. Spock had on society was the sabotage of parental authority. By being overly concerned with their children's psychological well-being parents overlooked the need for strictly observed rules, rules that set definite limits on behavior. The mistaken assumption running through Dr. Spock's interpretation of Freudian theory is that catering to the needs of the child as he progresses through the various stages of development will produce a well-adjusted child. When a child, disadvantaged by being wholly dependent upon his parents, is appropriately and sympathetically cared for, that child will come to know what his place is within the family. Furthermore, he will be eager to be a part of it by being unselfish and cooperative. Such is genuine self-discipline according to Freud, Dewey and Spock. The mistake in all this is putting the child at the center of the family by an overriding concern for his psychological needs. That gives the child the message that he is the center of the universe since his family is the sum total of his universe. This does not foster an attitude of cooperation. Nor does it produce a disciplined child. Rather, narcissism is the result. By believing that he is the center of the universe, the child has no basis upon which to develop respect for his parents much less anyone else. The undermining of parental authority leads to the challenging of it. And so we have the second nail in the coffin of values, the sabotage of parental authority thereby diminishing the values of discipline and responsibility.

> "For the very true beginning of her (wisdom) is the desire of discipline; and the care of discipline is love."
>
> The Holy Bible—Apocrypha 6: 17

CHAPTER THREE

Ethical Relativism

Values Under Attack: Moral Standards

A major cause of the moral decline of America has been the gradual acceptance of ethical relativism. **Ethical relativism** is the theory that there are no absolute or objective moral standards binding on all people. In other words, judging behavior as either right or wrong is simply a matter of opinion. There are two varieties: cultural relativism and subjective relativism.

Cultural relativism is a theory that has its roots in anthropology, the study of man. Human beings are social creatures and survive by living in groups. Consequently, anthropologists study group relationships and cultural history. The theory of cultural relativism was first publicized in the 1930s. It posits that different cultures possess different moral codes, that there are no absolute moral standards applicable to all people at all times. The extent to which any given action is judged morally right or wrong depends on the culture to which that person belongs.

No human being is born in a vacuum and therefore, no one can escape being born into some culture or other. The process of enculturation is an inevitable fact of life. It conditions an individual to be a reflection of his/her culture. The conventions of any given group determine to a great extent how an individual member of the group interprets his experiences with the world. The culture into which one is born literally shapes his view of the world.

Cultural relativism is the view that the truth or falsity of ethical statements is determined by cultural norms or standards. For example, euthanasia may be morally acceptable in Society A but morally unacceptable in Society B. Each society has its own set of moral codes and these vary from society to society. So the question of whether or not euthanasia is moral strictly speaking, has no absolute answer. If euthanasia is consistent with the moral code of a society, then the correct answer to the question is "yes." If euthanasia is inconsistent with the moral code of that society, then the correct answer is "no." All societies are governed by some moral code or other. That is a fact. And the determination of consistency, or lack thereof, of a specific activity with a society's moral code is one of fact. What cultural relativism rules out is any sense of meaning of the question, "Is euthanasia moral *per se*?" There is no extracultural standard by which to answer that question. Without any such extracultural standard, it is equally meaningless to ask "Which society, A or B, possesses the correct moral code?" There is no such thing as a moral code existing independently of society. Moral codes are culturally determined. Therefore, the truth or falsity of an ethical statement is culturally relative.

Subjective relativism is the view that morality is in the eye of the beholder. That is, morality is dependent on the individual, not society. Subjective relativism is an outgrowth of the ethical theory called emotivism. In his book *Ethics and Language* (1944) Charles L. Stevenson argued that ethical statements, such as "Keeping one's promises is good" are not statements of fact. Rather, it means a) "I approve of keeping promises" and b) "You do so as well." As such, a) is a statement about the speaker's attitude in regard to promise-making, revealing that the speaker is favorably disposed to promise keeping. Attitudes are the product of one's beliefs. When one thinks about it, however, the purpose of an ethical statement is more than a report of one's attitude concerning some type of behavior. It is also meant to convince the hearer to behave in a way consistent in this case with promise keeping and, therefore, b) is an imperative. Imperatives are directives concerning behavior. So the statement, "Keeping one's promises is good" means I approve of promise keeping and I think that you should too.

Ethical disagreements, then, boil down to disagreements in attitudes towards how one should or should not behave. It does not follow from this, however, that all ethical disagreements result in a draw or deadlock. One can always respond to the imperative aspect of an ethical statement by asking "Why?" The question, "Why should I keep the promises I make?" is a demand for some good reason or reasons for the behavior. Now, good reasons more often than not involve facts. For example, "You ought to keep your promises because if you do not, people eventually will not trust you and likely will not want to associate with you." Many, if not most, of the beliefs we have pertain to facts. So by supplying good reasons which themselves are fact-related the speaker stands a fair chance of changing the beliefs and therefore the attitudes of the listener. So long as the listener in the above example does not want to risk becoming a social outcast, the reasons offered by the speaker should be sufficient to convince the listener that he should also develop a pro-attitude toward promise keeping.

Emotivism gets it name from the imperative aspect of ethical statements. An imperative is only as good as its effectiveness. If one says, "Keep your promises." and no one behaves accordingly, the speaker has failed to get what he wants. The way to facilitate success in this regard is the use of emotionally-laden terms. Consider the emotive effect of, "Keep your promises, deadbeat." Emotionally charged words readily get people's attention and are most effective in getting changes in attitude. And getting agreement in attitude concerning behavior is the name of the game so far as an emotivist is concerned.

Subjective relativism evolved as a dumbed-down version of emotivism. A simplistic interpretation of emotivism equates opinions with attitudes. Furthermore, it is understood that an opinion is a value judgment. Now, there are only two kinds of statements; factual statements and evaluative statements and never the twain shall meet. Evaluative statements as expressions of value judgments are subjective whereas factual statements are objective. Facts are "out there" for everyone to see making possible common agreements as to what they are. Consequently, if a person claims that Rhode Island is the smallest state in the Union and another asserts that it is not, one of them must be mistaken *because* it is a matter of fact whether or not Rhode Island is the smallest state in the Union.

Since evaluative statements, however, are not expressions of fact, two people can have differing views without one of them being mistaken. Suppose two people are looking at the same painting. One says, "That's the most beautiful work of art I have ever seen in my life." The other responds, "You couldn't pay me to take it to the city dump." Is one of them mistaken? No, because there is no common; that is, factual ground for determining which assessment of the painting is correct. Both observers made value judgments, which by nature are subjective, about whether or not the painting is a good one. In this case, their judgments involved a work of art. Ethical value judgments are no different *in kind*. They are strictly subjective. So when two or more people have radically different views concerning abortion, for example, neither one is right or wrong in his assessment of it because morality according to subjective relativism is, in the eye of the beholder.

Many people have hopped on the bandwagon of subjective relativism. In *Death in the Afternoon* Ernest Hemingway wrote, "So far, about morals, I know only that what is moral is what you feel good after and what is immoral is what you feel bad after and judged by these moral standards, which I do not defend, the bullfight is very moral to me because I feel very fine while it is going on and have a feeling of life and death and mortality and immortality, and after it is over I feel very sad but very fine." (Scribner's, 1921, p. 4) Spoken as the devout narcissist that he was! And that point should not be lost. As Americans have become progressively narcissistic (see Chapter Nine) subjective relativism has become more and more attractive to them because it allows them to justify any and all behavior on the basis that one man's meat is another man's poison.

The adoption of ethical relativism has been a major contributing factor in the moral decline of America. It is my opinion that a reversal in the decline is not possible without a widespread rejection of ethical relativism. For this to occur, two things must take place: 1) people need to understand that ethical relativism reduces to absurdity and 2) something better must be offered to replace what's been lost. People will not accept their applecart being tipped over without having its contents being replaced by something better.

It is a fact of human nature that people have a need to feel good about themselves. This need cannot be met successfully unless they believe they are doing the "right thing." The "right thing" is the moral thing. The moral thing to do in any given circumstance is determined by the moral theory one follows. Demonstrating the absurdity of ethical relativism is relatively easy; successfully replacing it is, however, an altogether different and more difficult enterprise. In Chapters Eleven, Twelve and Thirteen, the weaknesses of ethical relativism will be exposed.

Cultural relativism has several weaknesses. First of all, it entails that reformers are always morally wrong since they seek to change the existing moral code of their society. Take, for example, the movement to abolish slavery in America. Since slavery was considered to be moral at the beginning of our country's history, then anyone advocating abolishing the practice *must be* morally wrong. Why? Because society (culture) dictates what is moral and not moral. Does this make sense? Were abolitionists morally in the wrong? Quite the contrary. They were morally courageous innovators willing to stand against the accepted moral standards of the day. Cultural relativism looks good in the abstract. Living by it in the face of institutionalized injustice is quite a different matter. Try to find a cultural relativist in a slave labor camp!

If that were not enough, there is a more basic problem with cultural relativism. The notion of culture is highly ambiguous and therefore notoriously difficult to define. What we speak of as Western Culture involves our cultural heritage extending all the way back to the ancient Greeks. European culture and American culture both are equally part of Western Culture. America itself comprises numerous subcultures. To further complicate matters, one person may belong to several subcultures. For example, abortion is not immoral in the United States and therefore is not illegal. But suppose Louise is an American citizen *and* a devout Roman Catholic. As a Catholic she is morally wrong to have an abortion but, as a U.S. citizen she would not be morally wrong in doing so.

How is this dilemma to be resolved from the standpoint of the cultural relativist? It would seem that the moral choice a person makes determines at that moment to which group or subgroup she belongs. Is this cultural relativism? Hardly. However, choosing as a Roman Catholic does not mean Louise is no longer a member of American culture. So what gives here? Well, the reality of the matter is that she makes a decision on the basis of what she is most comfortable with and then *justifies* it by reference to the moral code of one of the several subcultures to which she belongs. This is subjective relativism. And that is precisely the point. Cultural relativism inevitably reduces to subjective relativism.

Will subjective relativism withstand scrutiny? The answer lies in the purpose of morality. Moral codes exist primarily to assist people in resolving interpersonal conflicts and to promote the well-being of individuals within any given group. The interpersonal aspect of morality implies that there is more to moral decision-making than the satisfaction of ones' own desires. The subjective relativist makes room for the consideration of others only to the extent that it is in his own interest to do so. Basically, subjective relativism sidesteps the important element of interpersonal judgment. Second, subjective relativism altogether avoids the issue of the well-being of others. To wit; John might think that torturing people for the fun of it is OK behavior. As a subjective relativist he cannot be wrong. Ultimately, subjective relativism simply does not qualify as a *moral* theory. Nevertheless, an overwhelming number of Americans believe that subjective relativism is what morality boils down to. They agree with Hemingway that what is moral is what makes you feel good and what is immoral is what makes you feel bad, nothing more, nothing less.

Subjective relativism has two destructive effects. 1) No one's behavior can be morally right or wrong. Thus, any and all behavior can be justified no matter how depraved it is. The result of this is moral anarchy. Moral anarchy nets out to no morality at all. Consequently, any and all moral authority vanishes. 2) Because no one's behavior is morally right or wrong, it is illegitimate to sit in judgment of another person's behavior. This is the prevailing view today. We have become a country that frowns on those who make moral judgments pertaining to others. This would be reasonable if subjective relativism were reasonable. But subjective relativism is not reasonable. Judging other people's behavior as moral or immoral is part and parcel of holding people accountable and therefore responsible for their own behavior. Fortunately, there are moral standards that reasonable people can agree on (see Chapters Eleven, Twelve and Thirteen).

The widespread acceptance of **cultural relativism** and **subjective relativism** has greatly damaged the moral fabric of this country. These theories legitimize the unacceptable behavior of narcissists, namely the children described earlier who were raised in child-centered homes. The advent of the 1960s "flower children" was totally predictable. If no behavior can reasonably be judged wrong, there is no basis by which to take responsibility for it. The transparent greed of the 1980s was driven by self-interest and justified by subjective relativism.

> "The great man does not think beforehand of his words that they may be sincere, nor of his actions that they may be resolute—he simply speaks and does what is right."
>
> Mencius (372-289 B.C.), *Works*, bk IV, 2:11

CHAPTER FOUR

The Fifties

Values Under Attack: Courage and Integrity

In America, as we move into the 21st century, there seems to be a great deal of nostalgia for the 1950s, rooted in the belief that during that decade family values prevailed. Society was orderly, World War II was well behind us, we were the undisputed leader of the free world and our economy was strong. The family was stable, the rate of divorce dropped dramatically over the decade, few people locked their doors, and children were safe playing in the city park unattended. And there was no national drug problem. Dad was the breadwinner, Mom ran the household and together they raised respectful mannerly kids. And they all were God-fearing and went to church together. It was a period of tranquility when everyone had a defined role, took responsibility for their behavior and were happy. To a great extent this was made possible because people understood the value of conformity. Nostalgia, however, is the product of a selective memory. For all of its appearance of being an ideal time, the decade of the1950s was far from it.

First of all, the underlying mindset of the decade was an irrational fear of communism. This extreme fear of the Red Menace forced conformity onto the public at large. Conformity took several forms: political cowardice, the hypocrisy of middle-class values, and religiosity, namely ungenuine religiousness. The ever-present fear of Communist world domination led to the Cold War. The Cold War was sustained by an all-out arms race with ever increasing reliance on nuclear weapons. It was a time of profound underlying fear; the side with the fewest missiles reasonably fears total annihilation by the side with the superior arsenal. That's how peace was maintained. Peace was believed to be a function of superior force. Communists could not be trusted to keep the peace because they are irrational. Why? Because communism is anti-capitalist. Capitalism is the only rational economic system because it is good; that is, it produces good results. Consequently, any anti-capitalist system is evil and anti-American since America stands for capitalism. America represents good; communism represents evil. Americans are good; communists are evil.

In 1948, Czechoslovakia fell to communism and the Soviets blocked allied ground access to Berlin. The following year, the civil war in China ended with the communists in control. On top of that, the Soviets exploded their first nuclear weapon. In 1950, the Korean Conflict erupted compelling the United States to send troops in defense of the South Koreans who had been invaded by the North Koreans with the help of the Chinese. The conflict ended three years later in a frustrating stalemate.

These events fueled the American hysteria over communism and set the stage for the communist witch hunts led by Senator Joseph McCarthy. As chairman of the Anti-American Activities Committee, this reckless individual alleged that the United States government was riddled with communists as was academia and the entertainment industry. He went so far as to bully even his peers. In the process, he ruined the careers of many respectable people without ever being forced to provide conclusive evidence as to their guilt. The investigations of the accused were carried out in secret, often by paid informers. Judgments were rendered without the benefit of judge or jury. False accusation and innuendo provided a sufficient basis for condemnation. This went on for nearly five years until McCarthy became so outrageous that the Senate had no choice but to censure him. This occurred on December 2, 1954, after which he faded into obscurity. As deplorable as McCarthy's behavior was, we must not lose sight of the fact that he did not create the national paranoia over communism. He simply capitalized on it. And he was not the only powerful person in the commie-hunting business. In the long run J. Edgar Hoover, head of the FBI, was responsible for the abuse of the civil liberties of individual citizens to a far greater extent than McCarthy.

The hysteria over the Red Menace had two harmful effects on American society. 1) Civil liberties came under attack; not only did the government actively violate them, over half of Americans interviewed in a 1954 national survey agreed that all known communists should be jailed even if in doing so "some innocent people should be hurt." In addition, 78 percent of those questioned recommended reporting to the FBI neighbors and acquaintances believed to be communists. 2) Intellectuals were the target of witch hunting more than any other group. Even before McCarthy became a household word, the lion's share of anti-communist propaganda was directed against intellectuals. Even within the intellectual community itself, those whose views were not conservative often were berated by their colleagues as irresponsible. Under such pressure, most intellectuals took the path of least resistance. They avoided all causes such as civil rights for fear that they would be branded communists. Anything other than the status quo was suspect. Questioning the status quo became viewed as un-American. And anything un-American was communistic.

Since intellectuals to a great extent set the tone for society, it is they who must share the greatest blame for compromising their ideals and by not having the **courage** to take a united and public stand against such madness. They of all people knew better. They of all people could see through the irrationality of this Red scare and could recognize the maliciousness of McCarthy and his ilk. The intellectuals were the most cowardly of all.

In their zeal to expose communists, political conservatives went after the civil rights of activists, pacifists and atheists. This had a stultifying effect on any and all dissent. Keep your mouth shut and conform became the name of the game. That conformity became a defining feature of the fifties. Through their irrational fear of communism, the American public laid down and rolled over. They chose to forget the very principles upon which our

Republic was founded. They lost sight of the Bill of Rights. They abdicated their freedom and therefore were cowardly.

Due, in part, to the Red scare, the economy of the country thrived. The ensuing arms race gave rise to and fueled what Dwight Eisenhower dubbed the military-industrial complex. It fed the research, development and production of an increasingly sophisticated military hardware industry. Other industries driving the economy were oil, steel and the marriage between those two, the automobile. The latter profoundly influenced the configuration of the 1950s. Although the automobile had been around for a half a century, it was not until after World War II that cars became readily available to a great many Americans. The automobile provided mobility to its owners. Prior to this, mass transit such as trolleys provided transportation from neighborhoods to city centers and back. This limitation on mobility was a basis for community stability in the form of neighborhoods. Prior to the War, there was no genuine suburbia. The outlying areas of the cities were the domain of the wealthy in the form of estates.

Cars made suburban living accessible to the middle class. The development of suburbs was encouraged by the federal government. The Federal Housing Authority made home loans available to suburban home buyers. As corporate America flourished the prevailing wisdom was that successful internal promotion within a company necessitated a willingness by the employee to accept a transfer to a different locale. This greatly contributed to the demise of the traditional neighborhood. The traditional neighborhood had provided stability and fostered an attitude of responsibility and caring. Neighbors looked out for one another and shared the disciplining of their youth. But no longer did one grow up on Elm Street, graduate from the local high school, go off to college and return to enter the family business. Rather, a serviceman returned from the War and signed on to a corporation that transferred him to distant locales as he moved up the corporate ladder. The Federal Highway Act of 1954 called for a national interstate highway system and greatly contributed to the mobilization of America. In this process, the transferee located in suburbia of his newly adopted town because government financing encouraged him to do so. With transferee and his family fully expecting further corporate advancement and another move, no commitment was made to foster the bonds necessary to form a genuine neighborhood. An average suburbanite moved every three years. Annual moves were not unusual.

Although suburbia seemingly was an epitome of family values, it lacked the essential requirement of a genuine community which was and is the basis for establishing those values; most notably the looking out for the well-being of one's neighbors. Suburbia stressed the importance of the nuclear family but what we have learned is that reduction from the extended family to the nuclear family strips away many essentials of family values. Neighborhoods provide figurative extended families. The creation of suburbia was the death knell to traditional neighborhoods. As a consequence one of the sources of "family values" was compromised. To a great extent, becoming a transient society undermined our traditional core values.

Suburbia of the 1950s, was distinctly middle class. Its hallmark was conformity and that was the measure of all behavior. Differences not only were disapproved, they were judged to be deviant. Only the basic nuclear family was acceptable. Identical box-like houses were the norm with little or no variation in floor plan. Lots were of uniform size with no fences and few trees. Privacy was not only minimal, it was discouraged. Suburban inhabitants were expected to be joiners, giving rise to regular get-togethers such as backyard barbeques and evenings of playing bridge or canasta. This made suburbs appear to be traditional neighborhoods but underneath this facade of suburban stability there was systemic conflict that resulted in borderline schizophrenia that affected husbands, wives and children. For the husband, the breadwinner, it was required that he repress any sense of personal or professional individuality. He was expected to be the perfect organization man, a team player, a compromiser and most certainly one who never rocked the boat. Thrust by circumstance into suburbia via corporate transfer and craving community acceptance, he surrendered his core values. Peer reactions and status symbols were the standard by which he began to judge himself and others. The theoretical justification of such a compromise was cultural relativism; that is, that all values arise out of and are therefore determined by the community.

Just as injurious was the repression of the wives of suburbia. More than in any other period in American history, emphasis now was placed on wives giving undivided attention to the rearing of their children. A major contributing factor to this situation was Dr. Spock's emphasis on the child-centered upbringing of their offspring which demanded that women devote themselves full-time to the process. This demand had a profound influence on this generation of mothers. It literally became un-American for a mother not to define herself in terms of her children. Boredom was inevitable. Modern conveniences such as the washing machine liberated the housewife from chores that were otherwise time-consuming. Ironically, as the drudgery of the traditional woman's role decreased, the glorification of her role as housewife increased. Such glorification, however, rang hollow. Women were being told that they were men's equals. But in what sense? They were told that they were as smart as men and as capable of attaining college degrees. Yet, when they graduated with a degree in hand, comparable job opportunities were unavailable to them. Married or unmarried college-educated women were caught in a bind. If a woman was married, she was expected to be happy raising her kids regardless of her educational background. If she was unmarried, she was clearly a nonconformist. As such she should be encouraged to undergo psychotherapy to come to an understanding that her nonconformity was actually an abnormality. If she persisted in her desire to work, she should graciously accept a position that was noncompetitive with men. In other words, women competing with men was off limits. In fact, such competition was considered un-American and therefore deviant. In addition, the prevailing view was that the working mother posed a serious danger to her family. Without her full attention to her children, they were at grave risk of becoming homosexuals, juvenile delinquents, atheists, communists, any sort of deviant imaginable. This wholesale repression of women during the 50s was the reason why the women's liberation movement that began in the 1960s was so vitriolic.

Suburban children of this period suffered from their own form of schizophrenia. On the one hand, they were the first generation brought up under the guidance of Dr. Spock. The heart of such child-centered development is the glorification of the uniqueness and individuality of the child. On the other hand, these children were being raised in an atmosphere of conformity; their parents conformed to the roles expected of them. Things simply did not add up.

By the time these suburban kids got to college in the 1960s all hell broke loose. Through diligence and hard work, the parents had economically liberated their children. This gave their offspring the leisure time to step back and observe the status of American society once they arrived at college. What they observed they didn't like. They saw systemic hypocrisy throughout the society as evidenced particularly by the abuse of the civil rights of blacks and the suppression of women. They resented the imposition of university rules which they considered to be outdated. Many of them came to the conclusion that the Vietnam war was immoral and that the United States had no business being there.

The decade of the 1950s saw a significant return to religion. This was mainly due to the Cold War and the insecurity brought on by the existence of the hydrogen bomb. The fear of annihilation understandably drove people to the sanctuary of the church. But it went beyond that. Communists were our enemies and they were atheists. Consequently, religion came to be understood as necessary in the fight against communism. Religion and patriotism became synonymous; the religiosity of the fifties became good politics. As Senator McCarthy proclaimed: "The fate of the world rests with the clash between the atheism of Moscow and the Christian spirit throughout other parts of the world." And J. Edgar Hoover urged that "Since Communists are anti-God, encourage your child to be active in the church."

Although the church was considered to be a primary source of family values, this was obscured by the politics of conformity. Being an acceptable member of the middle class required that one be a member of a faith, most particularly Protestant, Catholic or Jew. Because this membership came from the external pressures of conformity, religiosity was the result. The underlying reason for the increased return to religion was an artificiality, one that the children of the middle class eventually came to see as hypocritical. Young adults who continued to attend church once they left home saw religion as a vehicle for social reform. This, of course, requires social activism which was anathema to their parents and society.

The religiosity of the period revealed itself via the popularity of Norman Vincent Peale. Although he was a preacher, his message was not a religious one. His books and sermons were "how to" manuals such as "How to Feel Alive and Well" and "The Key to Self-Confidence." His message was twofold: 1) the key to happiness is positive thinking. We "manufacture our own unhappiness" through "negative thinking." 2) One can attain a positive attitude by simple steps, rules or formulas. The response Peale generated was phenomenal. Such popularity can be explained, in part, by the frustration seething beneath the surface of the middle class. Being an organization man did not make Daddy feel alive and well. Mom, living with the doublespeak that she was man's equal yet told she was a social deviant if she wanted to do anything other than settle down in suburbia and only raise kids, had difficulty maintaining her self-confidence. Peale's message was safe because it was delivered from a pulpit. He was a churchman. His message, however, was anything but religious. Arguably, it was blatantly materialistic. One ad for his book *The Power of Positive Thinking* asked "ARE YOU MISSING THE LIFE OF SUCCESS?"

The increase in the return to religion during the 1950s was a phenomenon that characterized much of what occurred during this decade of the fifties, namely overwhelming, suffocating, disingenuous conformity motivated by irrational fear. As such religiosity demonstrated a lack of **integrity** on the part of those who flocked to churches and synagogues. They were not being true to themselves. That a great portion of this church-going was hypocritical is verified by a decline in attendance once the country became resigned to the fact that communism was here to stay and that our imminent annihilation because of it was remote.

All in all, the fifties simply were not all they have been cracked up to be. Individual courage and integrity were compromised. Neighborhoods declined and the extended family became a thing of the past. Once the children of the 1950s went off to college, they felt not only liberated but righteous in their open rebellion against most sources of authority. From their perspective, such authority represented the status quo which they believed to be the epitome of hypocrisy.

> "If everyone were clothed with integrity, if every heart were just, frank, kindly, the other virtues would be well-nigh useless, since their chief purpose is to make us bear with patience the injustice of our fellows."

Jean Baptiste Moliere, *Le Misanthrope* (1666), Act V, sc 1.

CHAPTER FIVE

Student Rebellion and the Counterculture

Values Under Attack: Civility

It would be misleading and inaccurate to attribute the American youth upheaval in the 1960s to the baby boom, progressive education, Dr. Spock, the Vietnam War, civil rights, television or any other single factor. Its occurrence was due to more than a combination of these and other elements. It was the Zeitgeist, a distinct spirit of the time that provided the oxygen that sustained the fire of student discontent. Such occurrences as the Vietnam War and the civil rights movement simply fueled the fire.

Due to the baby boom, record numbers of young people were going off to college. Just as importantly, they were attending college under far different circumstances than had the previous generation after World War II. The parents of the baby boomers buckled down and worked hard so that their kids would have a better standard of living than they had experienced as youth during the Great Depression of the 1930s. It is an understatement to say they succeeded. They created an economic boom that liberated their offspring. The importance of this cannot be overestimated. The unprecedented economic prosperity significantly affected the outlook of baby boomers. It freed them from thinking of a college education simply as a meal ticket. It allowed them to perceive the university as a garden where ideas were to be cultivated rather than as a glorified trade school. Students had the leisure time to examine the society that had produced them. The economics of the time made it possible for students to be idealistic.

There is nothing new in each generation rejecting to some degree the path followed by the previous generation but the sixties were different times. The decade of the fifties had been one beginning with the McCarthy Hearings. Many Americans believed that motherhood and apple pie, the American way of life, was being threatened by communism. Their children, the baby boomers, had cut their teeth on the Cold War and now they wanted peace, not war. The "establishment" construed their political idealism as Marxist, radical, left wing. Nothing was further from the truth as can be seen from a portion of *The Port Huron Statement*, the 1962 ideological declaration of the Students for a Democratic Society (SDS).

> We regard *men* as infinitely precious and possessed of unfulfilled capacities for reason, freedom, and love . . . . Men have unrealized potential for self-cultivation, self-direction, self-understanding, and creativity. It is this potential that we regard as crucial and to which we appeal, not to the human potentiality for violence, unreason, and submission to authority. *The goal of man and society should be human independence; a concern not with image (or) popularity but with finding a meaning in life that is personally authentic* . . . .

Within this passage can be found the basis for student rebellion during the 1960s.

When the baby boomers flooded college campuses they quickly discovered that they had not escaped the reach of their parents. As they had with previous generations colleges and universities functioned *in loco parentis*; that is, "in the place of parents." This translated into reams of campus rules and regulations principally to uphold moral standards. Not only were dormitories segregated by sex, visitations were restricted to the weekend. Curfews were rigorously enforced. Those colleges that permitted visitations beyond the common lounge to dorm rooms required that the door be partially open at all times with enforcement of the "three-foot rule"—three of the four feet of a couple were required to be on the floor at all times. To some extent every aspect of student life was regulated—class attendance, dressing, drinking, fighting, swearing and so on *ad nauseum.*

In addition, students discovered that they had virtually no say at the institution they were attending. Curricula were inflexible, types of intramural sports were set in stone and at most public institutions a minimum of two-years participation in Reserve Office Training (ROTC) was mandatory. Baby boomers were enraged at all these requirements and restrictions. But why? Their predecessors had dutifully accepted them. The answer lies in the fact that baby boomers were the first generation to be raised by the guidance of Dr. Spock. They were **disdainful of conformity**. As the products of child-centered upbringing, they were closet narcissists until they got away from mom and dad. Once on their own their narcissism was fully unleashed. They were not about to be told what to do and disciplined for their noncompliance. Predictably across the country there were numerous altercations between students and college administrators. One such conflict gave rise to the Free Speech Movement (FSM) at the University of California, Berkeley. In 1964 at the beginning of the fall semester, a dean dictated that henceforth student organizations were no longer permitted to set up tables on campus to promote off-campus causes such as civil rights or to protest the Vietnam War. This was an attack on freedom of speech and the students were outraged. Students violated the ban, and formed the Free Speech Movement. President Clark Kerr responded by suspending eight of the activists. That action backfired, stimulating a semester of turmoil resulting in Kerr withdrawing the rule that started the fuss and leaving the Free Speech Movement intact. This was the first major student revolt of the 1960's.

The civil rights movement played an enormously important role in the decade of student discontent. It started in earnest on the afternoon of February 1, 1960, when four black students at North Carolina A&T College walked into the local Woolworth's in Greensboro, North Carolina, sat down at a lunch counter reserved for whites and ordered coffee. They were refused service yet remained in their seats where they stayed until the store closed at 5:30 p.m. One of them told the waitress, "I'll be back tomorrow with A&T College." Sure enough, the following morning about 30 students, all nicely dressed, showed up at Woolworth's, were again refused service and left after two hours. An even larger crowd including three white students from Greensboro College appeared the next day. By week's end, hundreds of black students from nearby campuses appeared. Police caused a ruckus by arresting peaceful protestors for "inciting a riot." Sit-ins spread rapidly across the south. A nonviolent tactic, it was met with violence from the white establishment. Significantly, these upheavals were televised and broadcast during prime time. One might reasonably argue that the civil rights movement would not have garnered national attention had it not been for its exposure on television. For the first time in years students began to question what America really stood for. How can this be the land of the free when segregation is alive and well?

By 1961 sit-ins had accomplished the integration of lunch counters and theaters in approximately 200 cities. With this success more black and white students joined the movement. This gave rise to the freedom rides, a tactic to reveal that southern states were ignoring an earlier Supreme Court ruling that segregated buses and terminals were unconstitutional in interstate travel. Two buses left Washington, D.C. bound for the South. Not until they reached Alabama did they meet with resistance. Angry crowds of whites armed with clubs, tire irons and blackjacks mercilessly attacked the riders. Undaunted, the activists organized a second freedom ride from Nashville to Birmingham. When the bus arrived in Birmingham, the riders were attacked by an angry mob of 300 whites armed with pipes and baseball bats. Once again the nation was able to witness these events during prime time television. People nationwide were outraged. Activists pressured President Kennedy, forcing him to uphold the law in the South. Within a year most interstate travel and facilities had been integrated.

The civil rights movement was just getting started. Black and white students nationwide felt a moral obligation to get involved. They had been raised during the Cold War where patriotism was stressed. Typically, they began each school day with the Pledge of Allegiance. They had been conditioned to believe that this was "... one nation under God, with liberty and justice *for all.*" The civil rights movement demonstrated that there is liberty and justice *for all whites.* To be sure, many of the older generation were disgusted by what they were seeing on television but they generally did not share the idealism of their offspring. A great many white middle-class college students took the civil rights movement most seriously and became an active part of it.

The civil rights movement brought into focus another form of intolerance. Many colleges prohibited interracial dating and many states had laws against interracial marriage. In the long run these barriers did not survive. Again, students had been schooled to believe that what Thomas Jefferson had declared was the truth, that all people are created equal. Furthermore, it was not the business of a college administration or state legislature to dictate to anyone whom they could date or marry. In essence, such restrictions flew in the face of liberty. Although most students did not engage in interracial dating, most did oppose prohibitions against it.

The Vietnam War contributed greatly to student unrest. America's involvement in Vietnam was justified by the domino theory; that is, if South Vietnam were to fall to communism, all of Southeast Asia would eventually be controlled by the communists. This possibility was unsettling to most Americans. We were in the midst of the Cold War. America was paranoid concerning communism. If Southeast Asia were to go communist, what would be next? The spread of communism could not be tolerated. Communism was a direct threat to the American way of life in particular and to the free world in general. It had to be contained.

College students nationwide were rather sanguine about the

country's involvement in Vietnam until 1965 when draft quotas increased dramatically. Then they began to call into question the presumed catastrophic consequences of South Vietnam becoming a communist state. They simply did not "buy it." Their attitude was, "So what difference does it make if southeast Asia goes communist?" This reaction was based on the disbelief that the free world would be adversely affected by such a collapse. Furthermore, there was an undercurrent of feeling that the United States had no business poking its nose into the affairs of another country. This was *their* war, Vietnam's civil war. Students began to protest. They, as well as their black brothers, were the ones being sent to Asia to die! For what? College students demanded a rationale for fighting in Vietnam. They considered America's involvement in Vietnam immoral. This was reinforced by daily television coverage of the war. They watched as America defoliated a country of peasants with Agent Orange and napalm. They watched a junior army officer justify the day's activity of destruction by claiming that, "We had to destroy the village in order to save it." This sort of irrationality contributed to what became known as the Generation Gap. The students of the 60's increasingly rejected the mantra "My Country, Right or Wrong" which was generally accepted by their parent's generation. They did not see themselves as unpatriotic although they were judged by others to be so. Demonstrations against the war worsened and draft dodging become commonplace.

The civil rights movement and the Vietnam War were sufficient to create a sense of alienation within this generation of youth. Mistrust of government began early in the decade when students saw blacks not only denied their constitutional rights but brutally beaten by local police when they attempted to exercise those rights. The effect this had on many college youth cannot be overemphasized. It laid the foundation for a loss of trust in government, a most important value concerning the cohesiveness of society. This lack of trust leads to disrespect of the values that define institutions. An essential component of the concept of government is that of law and order. When police were turned loose on peaceful demonstrators, students were witness to the government turning on its own people. So far as the students were concerned, when police were turned loose on peaceful civil rights demonstrators it was law and order self-destructing. From that point of view it is understandable how and why the police became commonly referred to as "pigs," an epithet of contempt and total disrespect. How can people be expected to trust and respect government when J. Edgar Hoover, the head of its principle law-enforcement agency—the FBI, calls Martin Luther King "the most notorious liar in the country" and claims that the Southern Christian Leadership Conference (SCLA) "was spearheaded by communists and moral degenerates"?

For reasons cited above the mistrust of government was reinforced by the Vietnam War. Even within the armed forces, dissent among the troops grew to unprecedented levels as the war dragged on. Never in army history had desertions been so high. An increasing number of Vietnam vets became protestors against the war later in the decade.

Although not all college students by any means became alienated from the establishment, a significant percentage did, enough to leave an indelible mark on American society. They formed what became known as the counter-culture. Members of this counter-culture movement not only distrusted their government but called into question the values that had shaped America's institutions and economy. The Puritan work ethic and attitudes toward sex and marriage came under scrutiny. It was the work ethic that had built the greatest economy known to man. It was materialism in all its glory. Counterculture folk called hippies began to question the value of materialism and the ethics of capitalism. How, for example, can a company ethically manufacture napalm, a highly inflammable liquid, for the specific military purpose of torching a country (Vietnam) by air? How can the establishment justify its racial hatred and warmongering? The reaction was alienation and total rejection of establishment values. This rejection was expressed in catch phrases as "MAKE LOVE, NOT WAR," "QUESTION AUTHORITY," and "DO YOUR OWN THING."

"Make Love, Not War" represented not only a rejection of American militarism but of strict and "up-tight" sexual mores as well. Free love became commonplace among members of the counterculture. Fundamentally, they were seeking liberation from established values. "Question Authority" meant any and all authority. There is only one authority, the authority you have over yourself. "Do Your Own Thing" took on many forms. The LSD guru Timothy Leary recommended that people "Tune in, Turn on, Drop out." Tune in to yourself. Don't look to society to determine for you what is meaningful. You can only find that by searching your own soul. The disenchantment with the values of society led to much soul searching in an effort to replace what had been lost. Consequently, there became interest in Zen, astrology, Hare Krishna and Taoism.

"Turn on" referred to drug use—most particularly hallucinogens and psychedelics, to heighten awareness and simply to get stoned because it felt good. When society criticized this behavior it only reinforced the already existing alienation. How hypocritical can the establishment be? Mom is on uppers and downers and Dad comes home after work and knocks down a tumbler full of martinis. Nobody criticizes them!

Young people were urged to "drop out" from the mainstream and thereby reject the establishment. The establishment is hypocritical and phony. To conform is to be untrue to oneself. Many people who "dropped out" formed their own communities or communes to create self-sufficiency independent of the remainder of society. All of these attitudes and events of the 1960's and early 70's had an indelible impact upon American society. Terry Anderson speaks to this:

> Surveys by David Yankelovich Group in the early 1970's, confirmed in the late 1980's by Peter Hart Research Associates, found that the combined events of civil rights, campus activism, antiwar campaign, women's liberation, and the counterculture eventually altered the ethics of about 30 million people. The Sixties culture is different from their parents. They are more skeptical about experts, leaders, politicians, and about institutions—the church, government, and military. They are more flexible, introspective, and tolerant especially concerning race, living

arrangements, and personal behavior. They are more open about their feelings, and more liberated sexually. Women feel that they have the same right to sexual satisfaction as man, as demonstrated by a revolution of opinion about premarital sex: The double standard is dead. Even during the conservative 1980's, numbers soared of interracial marriages, gay couples, and single men and women living together. Cohabitation and other alternative living arrangements are common. Being "normal" is no longer a mandate for behavior: be yourself. Sixties people are more interested in self-fulfillment, defining their own lives, and they often question authority and do their own thing: let it be. (Terry Anderson, *The Sixties*, pp. 220-21.)

One would be hard pressed to criticize this generation's outrage over the treatment of blacks and of the government turning a blind eye to their civil rights. Criticism of the Vietnam War opened the public's eye to the unconscionable behavior of the federal government and it set a precedence for public scrutiny of future military campaigns. Consequently, the executive branch of our federal government is very cautious of committing U.S. troops abroad.

One question remains to be answered. Notwithstanding the civil rights movement and the Vietnam War, why were the youth of the Sixties disposed to question authority in the first place? *In loco parentis* regulations, for example, had gone unquestioned for previous generations of college youths. The answer lies in the effects of progressive education and ethical relativism. The Sixties generation to a great extent had not been taught to respect authority and ethical relativism provided the theoretical justification to do your own thing. In rejecting the hypocrisy and values of the establishment this generation threw the baby out with the bath water. The baby was **civility**. Manners became viewed as phony gestures. It was "cool" to be outrageous in dress, language and lifestyle. Vulgarity became commonplace. This was the beginning of the end for civility and manners in America. And it was a most unfortunate byproduct of this generation's rebellion. Manners are vitally important because they are the daily ways by which people demonstrate respect for each other.

Drug use and sexual promiscuity were not confined to participants of the counterculture. Regardless of one's moral stance concerning such behavior, it is clear that these activities have permanently altered the character of our society. Within the middle class, recreational drug use has become nearly as acceptable as liquor consumption. Among the underclass drug use has reached epidemic proportions. This expanded drug use has increased crime resulting in a public demand for stiff penalties for possession and for intent to sell the stuff. These stiff penalties include mandatory jail time. The result is that much of the present prison overcrowding is due to drug offences. This has led to the need for more prisons putting greater pressure on the states' budgets. Typically, this has resulted in an ongoing decrease in the allocation of monies for education. When this occurs society as a whole loses.

On May 9, 1960, the U.S. Food and Drug Administration announced approval of Enovid, an oral contraception for women. By freeing women from the age-old fear of pregnancy, the Pill indelibly altered the relationship between men and women by undermining the double standard. The Pill provided women with the sexual freedom men had always enjoyed. The Pill was the cornerstone for the success of the women's liberation movement that exploded onto the scene with the publication in 1963 of Betty Friedan's book *The Feminine Mystique*. This book was, to a great extent, a reaction to the oppressive expectations placed on women during the previous decade. The women's liberation movement also addressed women's civil rights issues including the landmark Supreme Court decision of *Roe v. Wade* guaranteeing a woman the right to an abortion. The movement has had continuing success in breaking down barriers to segments of the work place historically reserved for men running the gamut from long-haul truck driver to attorney to business executive to surgeon. In addition, there has been a continuous, if not frustrating, push for equal pay for equal work. Although the work of the women's liberation movement is not complete, the Pill opened the door to a whole new world.

"At some level, there is a substantive dimension to civility—a dimension that suggests itself when one thinks of civility's etymological cousin, *civil society*. The virtue of civility whether in public or private life, is a significant measure of an individual's capacity for self-government."

Steven Hayward, *Bush So Far On Principle*, V9, n4 (August 2001)

CHAPTER SIX

Vietnam

Values Under Attack: Trust in Government and Patriotism

The Sixties was truly an explosive decade in America. There was the Civil Rights Movement, the Counterculture and Student Movements, the Women's Liberation Movement and the Vietnam War. Each of these causes had tentacles that intertwined with the others but not to the extent that the identity of each movement was ever misunderstood or confused. They did, however, have one thing in common, television coverage. This more than any other factor fanned the flames of dissidence and discontent activating these crusades.

Prior to the Vietnam War the government could obscure the truth concerning the wars it fought because live television coverage was not available. The printed word can never convey the horrors of war as effectively as television. Truly, a picture is worth a thousand words. In addition, Vietnam was the first war in which reporters were routinely permitted to accompany the military as they engaged the enemy and the press was not subject to censorship. Daily live coverage of the carnage over a seven-year period took a psychological toll on television viewers. It helped turn public opinion against the war. Live coverage could not be doubted or dismissed as biased since most news coverage was highly supportive of American involvement in Vietnam. This had an enormous influence on the "hawks," hard-line advocates of the war. Over time, it influenced them to soften their position to the point that by 1972, the last of the hawks had come to the realization that U.S. involvement in Vietnam had not been a success. Just as importantly, as the war dragged on, it became evident that there were huge discrepancies between what the government was telling the people about Vietnam and the facts being communicated by the media. Daily carnage was brought into the living rooms of Americans. Year in and year out they sat by their televisions and watched in horror the savagery du jour, the South Vietnam national police chief executing a young Vietcong captive by shooting him in the head in front of reporters and, of course, a steady visual diet of scenes of American youth being mutilated. Eventually, the public began to ask, "Is South Vietnam worth the price?"

The involvement of the United States in Vietnam dates back to the Eisenhower administration. Historically, Vietnam had been a French colony. Upon the defeat of the French at Dien Bien Phu in 1954, the country was divided in half with the communist leader Ho Chi Minh in control of the north. At the time, the United States was paranoid concerning communism. The basis of U.S. foreign policy was worldwide containment of communism. Concerning Southeast Asia, containment was articulated in the form of the domino theory; that is, if South Vietnam were to fall to communism, all of Southeast Asia would eventually be controlled by the communists, which would be catastrophic for the free world. There was great fear that Ho Chi Minh would try to extend his power to the south. With American help Ngo Dinh Diem had been installed as president of South Vietnam. This action was followed up by the arrival of a team of military advisors.

Diem was a repressive and corrupt ruler. After he refused to hold elections in 1956 as guaranteed by the Geneva Conference, many South Vietnamese sought to overthrow the Diem regime by forming a rebel army, the Vietcong. Not surprisingly, they sought and received assistance from the North Vietnamese. As John Kennedy settled into his presidency, it became clear that the Vietcong had grown in strength over the years, and that the only way to keep Diem in power was to beef up American presence. Without publicity, Kennedy increased the number of U.S. military advisors in South Vietnam from 1600 in 1960 to 16,000 by 1963. This deployment had little effect. Vietnam made news as Buddhist monks and students protested in Saigon the summer of '63. Upon Diem's orders, police fired into peaceful demonstrators, killing many. Hundreds of monks were jailed. The response to Diem's repressive policies was shocking to Americans. In front of television cameras one monk sat down in a busy Saigon intersection, doused himself with gasoline and set himself ablaze. More of the same followed. It became increasingly obvious in Washington that Diem had thoroughly alienated most South Vietnamese. During the autumn of 1963, Kennedy and his advisors held ten meetings to discuss the "Diem Problem." Declassified documents reveal that the President was frustrated with Diem and he wanted more U.S. involvement in South Vietnam leading to a successful prosecution of what had become a war against the Vietcong. Consequently, he secretly approved a plot to overthrow the President Ngo Dinh Diem. On November 1, 1963, a handful of generals of the South Vietnamese Army conducted a coup. Diem was captured and assassinated.

The next major deception of the American public concerned the events surrounding the Gulf of Tonkin Resolution. On August 3, 1964, the destroyer *U.S.S. Maddox* was attacked by torpedo fire from two North Vietnamese PT boats in the Tonkin Gulf. As reported in *The New York Times*, the official Defense Department statement said that the destroyer ". . . was on a routine patrol when an unprovoked attack took place in the Gulf of Tonkin." President Johnson termed the North Vietnamese attacks "open aggression on the high seas." The American public was not told that the *Maddox* had been engaged in a highly secretive intelligence-gathering mission, mapping North Vietnamese coastal and air defenses. This operation was not confined to international waters. The day before the attack on the *Maddox* the U.S. had conducted two attacks on North Vietnam. This was not an isolated incident but part of a military campaign launched early in 1964 to increase pressure on North Vietnam. South Vietnamese patrol boats had attacked the North Vietnamese island of Hon Me and two villages near the Ho Chi Minh Trail had been bombed by the Laotian Air Force. Is it any wonder that there was a response by the North Vietnamese Navy? It is unlikely that a reported second attack on the *Maddox* occurred at all. Nevertheless, it provided the rationale for the Gulf of Tonkin Resolution, a vague charter that gave the President constitutional authority to help the South Vietnam ally. Considering the shroud of secrecy surrounding the resolution and the significant amount of misinformation being disseminated concerning the facts of our involvement in Vietnam, it is understandable that Lyndon Johnson's approval rating soared to over 70 percent. Although the North Vietnamese attack on the *Maddox* was clearly retaliatory, the American public was deliberately led to believe that it was the U.S. ship that had been attacked and had responded by sinking the attacking PT boats.

The turning point in the war came in spring 1965 when the North Vietnamese attacked a small American base at Pleiku. Until then, the role of American troops was officially advisory. Pleiku changed that. The 25,000 soldiers stationed in South Vietnam received new orders; now they were allowed to conduct search and destroy missions. Later that year, U.S. troops engaged the enemy in the first major battle of the war at Ia Drang Valley. Although greatly outnumbered, U.S. forces dominated Vietcong and North Vietnamese troops with the assistance of massive air support. As a consequence, the Vietcong resorted to guerilla warfare for over two years. The problem facing the Department of Defense was convincing the American public that we were winning this war of attrition. Throughout that period, the American public was constantly told that U.S. troops were making headway and it was only a matter of time before we would prevail. Broadcast news from the field did not substantiate any progress despite these official pronouncements.

During the period between 1965-'68, although there was general public support for the war, students had begun to protest. There was a genuine generation gap developing. Those who had fought in World War II could not understand the lack of "patriotism" on behalf of the younger generation—their very offspring! The younger generation kept demanding a rationale for fighting in Vietnam. Demonstrations grew more widespread. Students burned their draft cards at rallies. Thousands dodged the draft by moving to Canada. Others maintained their student deferments by going to graduate school. Professors at the undergraduate level contributed to the antiwar effort by refusing to flunk students, allowing them to continue their studies and not be drafted. Still others moved off-shore since no one studying abroad could by law be drafted.

On January 27, 1968, Field Commander General William Westmoreland announced to the American public that the enemy has "experienced only failure" and predicted success in 1968. Three days later, on the Buddhist lunar new year, the Vietcong and North Vietnamese army regulars began their most massive assault of the war known as the Tet Offensive. Most towns and villages controlled by the South Vietnamese government, including the capitol Saigon, came under attack. Some 4,000 Vietcong overran the airport, the national radio station, the presidential palace and the courtyard of the U.S. Embassy. These actions as well as the offensive taking place at other locations throughout the country were televised. Most viewers were at the very least disturbed. Some were horrified to see the brutal door-to-door fighting in the historic city of Hue and the strafing of villages with napalm by U.S. forces. Television broadcasts highlighted U.S. helicopters machine-gunning peasants running below in rice paddies.

The American military response to the Tet Offensive was severe, bolstered primarily by massive B-52 Stratofortress strikes. The enemy suffered huge casualties and, after three weeks, retreated to the jungle and resumed their guerilla tactics. Although the American military won the battle of Tet technically, at that point the Vietnam War was lost psychologically. The Tet Offensive proved that Westmoreland's search and destroy strategy had failed. We were no closer to victory in 1968 than we had been in 1965. American casualties were continuing to mount and still the end of the war was nowhere in sight. And it was becoming increasingly obvious that the government had been deceiving the public concerning our progress over the years in the prosecution of the war. This was the beginning of the public's disillusionment with our country's involvement in Vietnam. *The New York Times* observed that "The American people have been pushed beyond the limits of gullibility." From *Newsweek*, The "U.S. must accept the fact that it will never be able to achieve decisive military superiority in Vietnam." And *The Wall Street Journal* warned that "everyone had better be prepared for the bitter taste of defeat." The tide of public support was changing. Before Tet, a majority of citizens supported their government's commitment to South Vietnam; after that, a majority opposed it. Several U.S. Senators began publically criticizing our involvement. The Senate Foreign Relations Committee held nationally televised hearings concerning the progress and legitimacy of the war. The military left these hearings bruised.

Of great significance was the decay, over time, of morale among enlisted military personnel. During 1971, the U.S. armed forces nearly collapsed. Desertions increased to a record high in army history. Some 25,000 thousand military personnel voluntarily took less-than-honorable discharges. For those who remained, discipline radically declined. Acts of disobedience were commonplace as was the use of drugs. The hatred of the war affected all branches of the military. And when they returned to the U.S., many veterans did not hesitate to criticize and demonstrate against our involvement in the war.

In 1967, Secretary of Defense Robert MacNamara had assembled a team of 40 researchers to determine how the United States became involved in the war in the first place. That was most telling. Two years after U.S. troops began combat in Vietnam, the Secretary of Defense was searching for reasons why we were there! This research produced *The Pentagon Papers*. These classified documents revealed the truth as to how the U.S. became increasingly entangled in Vietnam and how the American public had been deceived concerning that process. One of the researchers, Daniel Ellsberg, had become disillusioned with the war and his role in it. As a matter of conscience, in 1971, he delivered copies of these documents to *The New York Times* which along with *The Washington Post* published them. That was the last straw. *The Pentagon Papers* gave credence to those who had suspected duplicity, lies and deception on the part of the government. These documents shocked and bewildered the "My Country, Right or Wrong" crowd. As a consequence, the hawks were unable to maintain credibility for their conservative point of view. Between March and June of 1971, opinion polls indicated that only 15 percent of Americans favored continuing the war. Almost 60 percent thought U.S. involvement was immoral. Over 70 percent believed the war was a mistake and advocated our withdrawal from Vietnam.

Beyond the loss of both American and Vietnamese lives and shattered families, the Vietnam War did a monumental disservice to this country. The systematic and prolonged deception of the American public by its own government led to a cynicism concerning the trustworthiness of the military and the government that remains to this day. When a government doesn't act responsibly, its authority can reasonably be called into question and all citizens suffer. Distrust of government eventually leads to the sort of dangerous extremism we have seen of late in this country such as separatists and militia movements. Furthermore, trust in government is a value that is directly related to patriotism. **Without trust in government there can be no genuine patriotism.** In a very real way, Americans lost their innocence because of Vietnam. It engendered the cynicism concerning government that is still with us today.

Regarding the reaction of Americans following the events of September 11, 2001, it is not surprising that they were outraged and we saw an enormous outpouring of sympathy for the victims and their relatives. This frequently took the form of donations to charities. Compassionate behavior should not be confused with patriotism. We could expect people to act as they did in the aftermath of 9-11 if a massive earthquake had been the cause of bringing down the twin towers. Furthermore, that we saw a vast increase in the display of the American flag should not be construed as genuine patriotism. It is natural for people to rally after being attacked. Nevertheless, people soon figured out that their government had let them down by having taken a most lax attitude toward international terrorism for the past 25 years. People will fight to defend their country and their way of life. That is simple survival. Patriotism, on the other hand, involves a belief in and a commitment to government leadership. Such belief and commitment is founded on trust. Trust in the government simply no longer exists.

> "Our country, right or wrong. When right, to be kept right; when wrong, to be put right."
>
> Carl Schurz, Address, Anti-Imperialistic Conference, Chicago (Oct. 17, 1899).

CHAPTER SEVEN

The Corruption of the Legal System

Values Under Attack: Personal Responsibility

There is no doubt that we have become a victim society that sues at the drop of a hat. Yet this was not always the case. Up until the 1960s lawsuits were a relatively uncommon occurrence because the laws at that time severely limited the conditions under which a person could sue another person. Then, the laws governing contracts and torts were deliberately changed. The legal theorists who initiated it believed that such change would contribute to the common good. Well intentioned though they were, their manipulations of the law and the changes they succeeded in making have greatly encouraged litigation. Suing someone is basically an act of legal finger pointing. From the standpoint of values, when this practice becomes acceptable and successful, taking **responsibility for one's actions** is discouraged. When people do not take responsibility for their own behavior, the outcome is a dysfunctional society where basically anything goes. Any and all behavior is justified. "Don't blame me for vehicular property damage. Blame the bartender for over-serving me. And while we're at it, let's hold the distributor responsible (liable) for supplying the drinking establishment as well as the company that produced the liquor in the first place." Here, the underlying reasoning, which has been upheld by the courts of late, is that, "I'm a victim who had no control or decision-making part in the events that resulted in property damage." Is it any wonder that we have a crisis of values in this country? What else can be expected when so many people are unwilling to take responsibility for their behavior? In order to understand how the changes in the law came about, a bit of background is necessary. Laws in this country are classified as either criminal or civil. There are two categories of the civil law; contracts and torts. Contract law is the law of agreements and promises. Tort law is the law of accidents and personal injury. For centuries, these two categories remained distinct from one another and the practice of civil law was devoted primarily to that of contracts. A contract is a mutual agreement between two parties concerning goods and/or services and the payment therefor. Ideally, the terms of the contract are explicit so both parties to the contract have no doubt what is expected of each other. Once agreed upon, each party to the contract has a responsibility to fulfill his part of the agreement. It is when one party to the contract does not discharge his responsibility that a suit is justified. Responsibility is strictly limited to the terms of the contract. This indicates an enormous confidence in the ability of individuals to be aware of the hazards inherent in many of the goods and services they purchase. Hence, the admonition, "Buyer beware." It is the responsibility of consumers to be the risk managers of their own environment. If in the purchase of a lawnmower nothing of a spoken or written nature is stated concerning safety, all risks reside with the buyer.

Stage One:

In the late 1950s a small group of well-intentioned legal theorists observed that accidents are socially costly. It seemed reasonable to them that the law should seek to minimize such costs. To that end, responsibility for one's safety should not be that of the consumer, but of the providers of goods and services. The latter are those who can least painfully absorb the cost of injury due to accidents. So, by one court decision at a time, these renovators of the civil law and their disciples began rewriting the law of contracts by first shifting the burden of responsibility for injury from the buyer to the seller. Consequently, if in the purchase of a lawnmower nothing of a spoken or written nature is stated concerning safety, both the buyer and seller are to presume the best, not the worst. As such, the seller is responsible in the event of an accident. Thus began the dismantling of contract law and the rise of new tort law which up to that time had been limited in scope. This transformation of the civil law occurred over the course of two decades.

Stage Two:

In response to the shifting of responsibility for injury from buyer to seller, manufacturers began providing express disclaimers along with their products. As part of the sales contract, the manufacturer stated the potential dangers inherent in the operation of the product. In addition, it was stated that the manufacturer would not pay expenses incurred in case of injury while the product was in use. Therefore, an express disclaimer on a lawnmower might state that its use was potentially dangerous in that the blades could easily amputate fingers and toes. In this way the force of contract put the onus back on the buyer. Standardized contracts issued became progressively more complex as manufacturers tried to protect themselves.

Not to be daunted, the disciples of the reformers fought back in an effort to circumvent express disclaimers, scrutinizing them to death. One tactic was to argue that the disclaimer had not been overtly brought to the attention of the buyer. Another was to argue that an inconsistency existed between a) some verbal exchange between the buyer and seller and b) that the disclaimer itself was inconsistent thereby nullifying it. Yet another was that the contract was null and void because of some technical point. The disciples of the reformers won the battle. After all, the typical consumer cannot reasonably be expected to read the fine print of a standardized contract. These were judged to be documents designed to get large corporate sellers off the hook to the disadvantage of relatively helpless individual buyers.

Eventually, the courts threw out contracts altogether on the basis that no conceivable disclaimer of safety could be adequate. For all intents and purposes, a contract was no longer a valid agreement when issues of safety were at stake. So vilified were safety disclaimers that they were denounced as "unconscionable" and "contrary to public policy." By the end of the 1960s many centuries of law governing contracts involved in the sale of goods, for professional services and pertaining to employment had been completely dismantled. In an effort to protect the public, the legal wizards of change unwittingly set the stage for individual consumers to perceive themselves as **victims** of the corporate world. As such, they were no longer responsible for their own behavior. If anything adverse happened to the consumer, it was not his fault. Fault lay on the side of the provider.

Stage Three:

The death of contracts made it possible to hold the manufacturer totally responsible for the products he produced, including any product that was defective. At first, the new law of torts focused on manufacturing defects. This is restrictive because it pertains only to individual items produced. For example, if it could be shown that the blades on a certain lawnmower flew off because the screws had been improperly installed, this was a manufacturing defect. Such defects tend to be rare and pertain only to a single unit coming off the assembly line. That range of liability seemed too restrictive to the disciples of the reformers. In one momentous move, they extended the range of liability to cover defects in design. Design defects target the entire production of a given model of, say, automobiles. In the early 1970s, Ford Motor Company produced the Pinto. If rear-ended with sufficient force, the Pinto's gas tank would rupture and explode. This was a design defect. It seems most reasonable that the manufacturer ought to be held liable for it, especially if the company knew of the design defect from the get-go which, in this case Ford Motor Company did. Company officials had decided against the extra $10 per unit cost that would rectify the problem. This is a straightforward example of design defect. Manufacturers, however, are not always aware of design defects in their products. When a product fails, who is to say that the failure was the result of a design defect? The more complex the design, the more difficult it is to determine whether or not a defect is the result of design.

Stage Four:

Just who is to say whether or not a given product was designed defectively? Juries deciding personal injury cases cannot reasonably be expected to know the finer points of design. But experts can. So lawyers for both the plaintiff and defendant trotted into the courtroom expert witnesses of every conceivable kind. This, however, did little to resolve the quandary of juries. Eventually, juries came to realize that expert witnesses were nothing more than hired guns. Expert witnesses present two problems. 1) Since they are paid for their testimony, doubt can be raised as to their objectivity; after all, they are working *for* the plaintiff or the defendant. 2) Without an adequate background concerning a product's design, how can a jury determine which expert witness to believe? In the end, juries were still left scratching their heads in defect design liability cases.

Stage Five:

Even though the testimony of expert witnesses did not definitively affect juries, it certainly got the attention of a number of government officials and led to greater regulation of products and services. Such regulation is a dream come true for litigants because it creates the possibility of violations of the regulations. No matter how innocent or technical a violation may be, it becomes fair game in the area of torts. As time passed, even complete compliance with stated regulations could not withstand the onslaught of litigation. The courts judged compliance with stated regulations merely a minimum requirement concerning products and services. Stated regulations typically address only specific aspects of conduct, manufacture or design. That regulators did not anticipate every possible hazard facing the users of a given product and include it in the regulations simply indicated the inadequacy of the regulations. Consequently, if a product could be shown to cause injury *no matter under what conditions of use,* then the manufacturer could be held liable. Furthermore, the courts took the cynical view that the government agencies that originated such regulations were not to be trusted. They were either in the back pocket of the business community who they ostensibly regulate or they were career bureaucrats and therefore deadheads.

Part and parcel of government regulation is that the product must carry warnings by the manufacturer. Yet even when there was compliance to the letter (of the warnings), the courts sided with the plaintiff. For example, one Richard Ferebee contracted pulmonary fibrosis as a result of long-term exposure to a herbicide manufactured by Chevron. Chevron had scrupulously complied with the Environmental Protection Agency (EPA) in the warning label attached to its product which stated in large bold letters: DANGER, CAN KILL IF SWALLOWED, HARMFUL TO THE EYES AND SKIN. In addition, this label directed the user to immediately wash skin that had been exposed to the chemical and to remove contaminated clothing. The label also stated that "Prolonged contact" would cause "severe irritation." A jury and then a federal court of appeals decided that this was not enough warning because "it failed to mention the specter of long-term lung disease culminating, perhaps, in death." Despite this determination, the court conceded that Chevron had no legal right to add to or depart from the EPA's prescribed warning. That they were in complete compliance with the EPA regulation was of no consequence. Chevron could either petition the EPA for a change in the warning or continue to use the prescribed warning label and pay future successful suits against them.

Stage Six:

With specified regulations providing only necessary but not sufficient grounds for deciding tort cases, and the perplexity on behalf of juries concerning which expert testimony is ultimately credible, it is little wonder that the outcome was random and often downright incoherent; that is, judgments that defied common sense and were simply preposterous. In essence, the new law of torts had resulted in a sort of legal lottery. The producers of goods and services were now caught in a bizarre melodrama, never having a clue what the outcome of litigation against them might be even though they had complied to the letter of the law. As a result, rather than fight litigation, more and more companies have opted to settle up front to avoid the ever-increasing costs of defending themselves under an irrational set of circumstances.

Stage Seven:

The decision by producers of goods and services to settle out of court to avoid costly litigation has given rise to the number of frivolous lawsuits. And why not? What does a plaintiff have to lose? After all, there is no shortage of lawyers who will work on a contingency basis. Even if the case has no legal merit a lawyer only needs to win a few large judgments to be set for life. Since it costs the plaintiff nothing to sue, the stakes as well as the odds of winning, are far better than those found at a Las Vegas casino.

Given this evolution in tort law, is it any wonder why taking personal responsibility for one's own behavior has taken a huge hit? The legal system itself has contributed to the decline of values over the past forty years. It has literally aided and abetted the avoidance of personal responsibility and encouraged irresponsible behavior at the same time. Consider, for example, the egregious awards recently granted by juries to people who have sued the tobacco industry for damages due to the ill effects of smoking. Given the warning label that has accompanied each pack of cigarettes for several decades, anyone who does not realize that smoking is potentially cancer-causing qualifies as dim-witted. Anyone who smokes does so as an act of free will and should be responsible for whatever befalls him as a result of the choice he makes to smoke. It is reason run amuck to hold a tobacco company responsible for the lung cancer contracted by an individual who has smoked two packs of cigarettes a day for 40 years.

Manufacturers of products from ladders to sports equipment have literally gone out of business as a result of having been sued by someone who sustained injury while using their product even though there was no substantial proof of anything faulty with the product. An individual who disregards the warning not to stand with both feet on top of a ladder can sue the company if he is hurt falling off of it. Anyone who plays football or ice hockey knows that they are inherently dangerous sports. No matter, the manufacturers of helmets for such sports have been sued because of neck injuries sustained by individuals playing these games. Such examples are endless and they undermine the taking of responsibility for one's behavior and thus encourage a victim mentality.

Coincidental to the aforementioned changes in the law Americans generally have come to view themselves as victims, persons subjected to oppression, deprivation or suffering. The victim-ization of America knows no boundaries. And that's a big problem because it justifies the laying of blame on someone other than oneself. In other words, being a victim releases one from taking responsibility for one's own behavior. One can be a victim of race, ethnicity, gender, addiction, phobia, socio-economic status, physical disability, mental abuse, lack of self-esteem, you name it. Victimization is perfectly consistent with the child-centered upbringing recommended by Dr. Spock, concerned not with others but with the *self*. Being a victim justifies not accepting responsibility for one's behavior and, consequently, justifies any and all behavior no matter how extreme it may be.

> "Personal responsibility sets us free. Personal responsibility makes us self-reliant. Self-supporting. Thoughtful. Productive. Personal responsibility makes us prosperous and civil."
>
> Michael Cloud, Libertarian candidate for U.S. Senate, Massachusetts (February 15, 2002)

CHAPTER EIGHT

Television, Music And Hollywood

Values Under Attack: Respect for Religion, the Family and Other People; Decency

No one can reasonably doubt the effect television has had on American society. Television, however, is only one dimension of the entertainment industry in this country. To a great extent, what is on television is a reflection of the status quo in Hollywood. That which is projected onto the big screen eventually passes through the tube. Television is unique in the size of audience it can capture and influence. Television's conquest was swift. In 1946, there were only 7,000 television sets in use throughout the nation. By 1960, the number had grown to over 50 million. Today, the television is considered a home necessity. As omnipresent as television is, television programming is a justifiable concern for those who care about the possible effects it has on its viewers. And since a sizeable percentage of those viewers range from two to eighteen years of age, that concern becomes all the more pressing. It is an inescapable fact that television and film have become progressively violent and vulgar over the past 35 years. How and why has this happened?

How television and film degenerated in content has much to do with the film Production Code. Beginning in 1922, the major studios agreed to self-censorship regarding all offensive content of movies produced in Hollywood. This Code was formalized in 1930 by the Motion Picture Association of America. It placed specific restrictions on obscene language, ethnic insults, sex, violence, drug abuse as well as other offensive behavior in movies. The Production Code was respected by film producers until the early fifties when television became serious competition to the movies. In order to lure paying customers back to movie theaters, Hollywood producers began to bend the Code and subsequently break it. During this period, the public got its only glimpse of what quality television programming could be. During prime time the networks offered shows for widely disparate tastes. One could choose from among quality documentaries, live original dramas, opera, boxing, musical variety shows, situation comedies, adventure shows and news programs. By the mid-fifties, however, the programming became more and more homogenized due to pressure on the networks from sponsors and various interest groups. It was as if the Production Code had passed from one medium to the other; television would censor its subject matter, movies would be allowed to be more permissive and avant-garde.

Television network executives were cautious. They were not about to get crosswise with the anti-communist hysteria that was sweeping the country. Their fear was well-founded. In 1950, three ex-FBI agents published a book called *Red Channels* which detailed the justification and methods for systematic blacklisting. The network executives calculated that bland programming would be a safe way to avoid the spotlight. Consequently, television shows began to reflect the conformity that characterized the decade. (See Chapter Four.)

The network honchos also understood who paid the bills. Sponsors paid for television. The success of advertising was achieved by reaching great numbers of people. Sponsors calculated that they would attract the largest audiences by sponsoring shows that appealed to the lowest common denominator. They were correct and insipid programming carried the day. The public came to be seen by sponsors as a mindless herd to be manipulated for money and power. Television became nothing more than a commercial medium in the eyes of sponsors and network executives.

So, during the 1950s, fear and greed on behalf of the network executives ultimately dictated what was being offered to the viewing public. One would think that such a large audience could have had some say in the matter. Not so. Television functioned as a one-way street. Why? Because in the fifties, people trusted the leaders of both business and government. Trust in government is a value that was compromised as a result of the Vietnam War. (See Chapter Six.) Individuals audacious enough to object to the mediocre programming were either ridiculed as "highbrows" or told that they were free to change channels. This response was insulting. The freedom to change channels presupposed an acceptable alternative to tune into. There wasn't an alternative and that was precisely the problem.

By the end of the decade the variety of television shows that had sparked the beginning of it was nonexistent. The network executives simply did not live up to their social responsibility. Had they resisted the urge to accumulate massive wealth and personal power they could have discharged their responsibility to the public by offering a higher caliber of programming and some honest choices to boot. But by so doing, the sponsors would never have attained such an enormous influence over the medium. The network executives of the fifties lost sight of the fact that social responsibility is in direct proportion to the amount of power one has to influence the public.

Television of the fifties was not devoid of violence. Such shows as "The Untouchables" and "Hawaiian Eye" threw violence into the mix. However, it was always in the context that the bad guys lose and the good guys win. At the outset, the potential adverse effect that gratuitous violence had on children by way of television was an issue but a relatively minor one. Resolving disputes through dialogue has never been an American trait. Our mode of problem solving historically has been, "If you can't buy it, shoot it." So it is no surprise that early televison action shows featured violence. Furthermore, since vulgar language and sexual references were forbidden, violence become the sole means to spice up otherwise inane shows and keep viewers from turning off the tube altogether. The debate over the cathartic value of gratuitous violence versus its potential to cause aggressive and violent behavior continued.

In Hollywood, the subject of debate was the Production Code. Even though it had eased somewhat, some producers felt that it unjustly restricted their creative potential. Defenders of the Code argued that adherence to it was necessary to avoid alienating the viewing public. The debate ended when Jack Valenti became the president of the Motion Picture Association of America in 1966. His first action was to suspend the Production Code. After nearly 40 years Hollywood was free at last. From that point on movie producers have portrayed on the screen ever-increasing amounts of material that is degrading to humanity and assaults institutions that the average American values such as religion and the family. Television lagged behind the motion picture industry in the frequency and intensity of offensive material. But it was only a matter of time before it caught up.

Since the advent of MTV in 1981, the music and television industries have kept pace with Hollywood in the production and dissemination of offensive material. Iconoclasm, baseness and vulgarity along with extreme and excessive gratuitous violence and demeaning and explicit sexual behavior are everyday television fare. One cannot help but wonder why this is the case. The entertainment industry answers this question by steadfastly maintaining that what it produces is simply a reflection of the society at large, that they produce nothing that is not already a reality. The industry claims that it is simply reflecting in an honest and artistic way the ever-increasing baseness of and violence in our society; they are only the messengers delivering the bad news.

On the surface, this response seems plausible. However, it is factually incorrect. For example, crime rates have gradually but steadily declined over the past 20 years. Nevertheless, over that same period of time, violence portrayed by the entertainment industry has risen almost exponentially. And it does more than recreate real-world violence. It glorifies it by creating heroes out of brutish characters, reinforcing the view that brute force is not only the best but the only way to solve problems. Although the vast majority of Americans value marriage, film and television producers often cast it in a negative light. The movie *The War of the Roses* is a case in point and even though most Americans are religious adherents the entertainment industry has over the years routinely maligned and distorted organized religion. Good examples are the movies *The Last Temptation of Christ* and *Cape Fear*. The point is that when representatives of the entertainment industry assert that its products reflect the status quo of society, they are factually wrong.

In response to the concern that the antisocial behavior depicted in movies, television, MTV and music has a negative causal effect on the public in general and some individuals in particular, industry officials have staunchly maintained that there is no conclusive scientific data proving that to be the case. Again, they are factually mistaken. Since the mid-seventies, psychologists and law-enforcement officials have systematically confirmed the damaging effect of entertainment brutality. Such studies are numerous. To argue that a constant barrage of violence has no effect on viewers and listeners defies common sense. No one seriously doubts that television is a powerful educational medium. It successfully educates by repetition as amply demonstrated by *Sesame Street*. There is power in redundancy and everyone knows it.

Why, then, would anyone deny the redundancy effect of violence? The underlying reason for such denial by the entertainment industry is that they don't want to be regulated. One way of stonewalling is to deny any causal link between a given violent movie or tape and a crime committed by a specific individual. To prove such is difficult indeed. But this sidesteps the issue; it ignores the accumulative effect of watching and/or listening to violence over an extended period of time. Seeing one violent movie probably is not going to cause someone to commit a crime. The studies prove, however, that a consistent diet of violence will. Furthermore, there is ample evidence that exposure to constant violence desensitizes especially children and young adults. The net effect of this is that as violent images get progressively extreme, the less people are disgusted by them and the more likely they are to accept violent behavior as the norm.

> ... Humans are aroused by and interested in ideas and events that are moderate transformations of what is familiar. In a society where most people believe that the majority are law abiding and not planning robbery, rape, murder or child abuse, reflection on these asocial acts elicits some anxiety and we do not dwell long on these ideas. Hollywood does not make expensive movies about cannibalism or a father sodomizing his son because those scenes would bother most Americans. But dishonesty, torture, murder, arrogance, deceit, and narcissism, which are always with us, are being cleansed of some of their earlier moral revulsion. The prevalence of these behaviors has permitted Americans to think about these acts and to pass from a state of aversion, terror, or disgust to one of curious interest. These themes now sit in a narrow space characterized by uncertainty. They titillate us in the same way that films filled with carnal sex did in the 1960s.
>
> (Jerome Kagen, *Three Seductive Ideas*, p. 168.)

Further stonewalling by the industry is demonstrated by its argument that any regulation would violate the First Amendment right to free expression. This claim is highly questionable. If one cannot escape such "entertainment," then a case can be made for the violation of one's privacy. The industry's response to this is: "If you don't like what you see on television, simply turn it off. If you don't like violent and foul movies, don't go to them." "If you are disgusted by the lyrics of some song, don't listen to it." That is all well and good except for the fact that the vulgarity, violence and irresponsible sex is so all-pervasive that realistically a person cannot escape being assaulted by it. Furthermore, it is impossible for parents to shelter their kids from exposure to it. A child would have to be raised in a bubble to escape the effects of television and popular music. Yet the movie moguls and network executives simply don't care.

So why don't they care? The answer lies in the type of people attracted to the entertainment business. It is a haven for narcissists. Public adulation of entertainment "stars" makes the business very attractive to narcissistic individuals. The money and fame feeds the narcissistic needs of them all. To acquire more adulation, money, power and fame the industry panders to the narcissistic elements of its audience, the viewing public which, in turn, gives the industry more of what it wants. This develops into a vicious cycle, each revolution of which presents a more extreme product than before. That is why the violence and sex in movies and on television has become increasingly extreme. Each production has to outdo its predecessor by being more and more sensational.

That a sizable percentage of the viewing public has been turned off doesn't seem to matter. Producers and directors have convinced themselves that they are artists on the cutting edge of social commentary. But why is the content of that commentary almost always on the dark side of human nature? The answer once again is found in the narcissism of Hollywood. Narcissists tend to be shallow people. As such, they have difficulty dealing with or exploring the complex side of human nature and the depths of meaningful and rewarding social interaction. Consequently, contemporary Hollywood heroes are cool, aloof and invulnerable. That's macho. And macho characters settle disputes by brute force. They don't love. That would make them vulnerable. They substitute sex for love. Macho is studly. Actors are well suited to the shallowness of this brand of social commentary. To quote Madonna, "The actors and singers and entertainers I know are emotional cripples. Really healthy people aren't in this business."

All forms of media cater to the public's innate narcissistic tendencies by displaying the Hollywood lifestyle as exciting and glamorous and public demand is strong. From *People* Magazine to television's *Entertainment Tonight* people flock to live vicariously through the "beautiful people." What they see is an ostentatious display of wealth and glitz in all its superficiality and shallowness.

So the entertainment industry feeds its viewers a diet of vulgarity, sex and violence on the one hand and superficiality on the other. In light of this, how can concerned citizens be expected to withstand the entertainment industry's continuous assault on religion and the family? What can we do to counter the disregard for common decency and the inappropriate portrayal of how we ought properly resolve interpersonal conflicts? Although it is within our power to avoid going to movies, it is totally unrealistic to think that we can escape the tube. The only defense the public has is in the choices individuals make concerning their own behavior. We have the ability to discern vulgarity from civility. We can choose to resolve our disputes in a civilized manner rather than resorting to violence. Behaving in such a way becomes all the more important in setting examples for our offspring. Children emulate their parents' behavior and studies have shown that parental behavior is of greater influence on children than what they assimilate through television. So it becomes all the more pressing that parents function as models of behavior so that movies, television, MTV and music do not set the behavioral standard for their children. We are obligated to society, ourselves and our children to be nonviolent, to treat sex as a byproduct of love, to be civil and forsake crudity because vulgarity is degrading to humanity. Only by taking it upon ourselves to be living examples of decency can we challenge and overcome the insidious effects that the entertainment industry has brought to bear on our society over the past 40 years.

"A man's real life is that accorded to him in the thoughts of other men by reason of respect or natural love."

Joseph Conrad (1857-1924), *Under Western Eyes* (1911), Pt I, chapter 1.

CHAPTER NINE

The Age of Narcissism

Values Under Attack: Concern for Others and Unselfishness

The notion of narcissism comes from Greek mythology. Narcissus was a Greek god who found his ultimate pleasure in gazing upon himself. Hence, 'narcissism' means self-love. Narcissistic individuals are egocentric, which every human being is to some extent. In fact, our survival depends on it. The issue is one of balance. It is when our narcissistic tendencies rule our behavior that problems arise. To a great extent, we have become a narcissistic society. This has occurred during the last half of the 20th century and is due primarily to the breakdown of the family unit. The steady increase in divorce is most often cited as the cause of this breakdown. Divorce pertains to the breakup of the family unit; that is, the formal splitting apart of families. The breakdown of the nuclear family occurs when the family becomes dysfunctional. There are many dimensions of dysfunction but there is not necessarily a connection between them and divorce. Among other things, children in dysfunctional families typically lack self-esteem. As such, they are disadvantaged when attempting to fit into society at large. This creates frustration, anger, and sometimes results in violent behavior. It makes adult relationships difficult to establish and maintain. In the end it makes happiness elusive. Typically, such people unwittingly substitute greed for happiness thus reinforcing the demands of a completely narcissistic individual. The causes of a dysfunctional family are best understood by exploring the nature of a family and how children ideally are raised.

A family is a miniature society. It functions as a social institution with rules and regulations and is guided by moral values. The family provides the environment wherein a child is socialized. Narcissism characterizes the infant at birth and understandably so. His world contains only one person. His narcissism is reinforced because he gets what he wants when he wants simply by crying. His first impression of life is that the satisfaction of his needs are all that is important. After all, everyone **he knows** has been most accommodating. This self-centered existence eventually comes into conflict with the needs of other members of the family. At this point the child's socialization training begins. It is designed to teach him that he is not the center of the universe. Rather, he is but one part of a unit and consequently must conform to and abide by the rules and regulations of the social unit of which he is a member. Restraints are progressively placed on him for the purpose of training him to control his natural narcissistic tendencies. It is a continuous battle between parent and child which evolves into an ongoing negotiation. "Relinquish your selfish inconsiderate, narcissistic ways and you will be rewarded. Persist in them and you will be punished." Such childhood training is seen as successful when the child makes the transition from a primarily narcissistic human being to a social person who is appreciative of the needs of others.

Such a socialization process does not mean the elimination of conflict. Rather, it sets the stage for a lifelong internal struggle to curb one's natural narcissistic instincts in consideration of other people's needs. That this is a struggle does not mean that it is an impossible one to resolve or that one's own needs are never met. It means developing self-control guided by a moral conscience. The above-mentioned transition involves a change in attitude; from behaving properly for fear of punishment to so behaving because one understands that it is simply the right thing to do. Throughout this process, the child learns that exercising self-control is a necessary component of acting responsibly. As a child assumes more and more responsibility for himself and his actions, the greater is his self-esteem. It is crucial to understand that self-esteem can only be earned; it cannot be given. A critical aspect in the development of self-esteem is coming to terms with one's limitations. One cannot possess self-esteem unless he possesses an honest understanding of his weaknesses as well as his abilities. Such an understanding is necessary for an individual to develop a real sense of self-worth. Children see through false praise. They want and deserve honest evaluation of their performance. Self-esteem is acquired by honesty, hard work and persistence. Encouraging a child to do for himself not in a selfish way but in terms of testing his mettle provides the foundation of a successful independent person. A person cannot be truly successful without independence or autonomy for without autonomy one is always dependent on others either mentally or physically in a needy way.

A child-centered home is one of the root causes of a dysfunctional family. It prevents the child from developing self-esteem because he has a false sense of his proper role in society beginning with his role within the family. He is taught that he is special which lessens the expectations of him and caters to his natural narcissistic nature. This inevitably leads the parents to do more for the child and in the process rob him of the opportunity to learn to do for himself. Without learning to do for himself, he learns neither self-worth nor responsibility. The image of himself as something special ultimately thwarts his success as he enters society as a teenager because he has never developed an understanding of his limitations. This creates an insecurity in terms of his presumed abilities for competing in the world at large. To maintain his sense of being special, he limits his choices to fit his narcissistic needs. When he experiences defeat, it is always someone else's fault; he sees himself as a victim. He has never been taught to take responsibility for his own behavior and this carries over into his adult life. His child-centered upbringing never taught him to persevere in the face of failure and therefore to never experience true success. As such he has little or no self-esteem for self-esteem cannot be given, it can only be earned.

Such a person enters into relationships not as an autonomous, fully responsible adult but rather as an immature person desiring to satisfy his narcissistic needs. Such is not the stuff of which successful marriages are made. Not surprisingly, divorce runs high in such unions because they are built on selfishness, not selflessness. Immature and narcissistic parents are hardly adequate role models for their offspring. Never having been taught self-discipline, they lack the tools to raise their children with this quality. Furthermore, because children are great emulators of parental behavior, the natural narcissism of the child is reinforced. And so a vicious cycle is perpetuated.

What seduced parents into child-centered upbringing? The first factor was Dr. Spock's book *The Common Sense Book of Baby and Child Care*, originally published in 1946. (See Chapter Two.) This book became the bible for child rearing for decades. Although Dr. Spock always emphasized the importance of discipline, that message was lost; his psychoanalytic and Freudian approach to child rearing was interpreted by his readers as permissiveness.

A second factor contributing to child-centered home environments is affluence. Beginning with the 1950s, the standard of living in our country began to rise and continued to do so throughout the remainder of the century. We became the Affluent Society. The childbearing generation of the '40s and '50s had gone through the Great Depression as well as the Second World War. They were determined that their kids would be "better off" than they were. They succeeded in upgrading their material status and therefore that of their children. In fact, they economically liberated their offspring which made possible the leisure mentality they took to college.

Affluence contributed to the creation of the counterculture, the hallmark of which was narcissism. Do your own thing by tuning in, turning on and dropping out. This behavior was perfectly consistent with the child-centered way in which the '60s generation had been raised. "Turning on" to drugs became commonplace increasing to such proportions that it is presently a national crisis. Addiction, be it drug addiction or any other form of addiction, is an expression of narcissism. The "drug," crack cocaine or chocolate, is only the means to the end of self-indulgence. Self-indulgence is the essence of narcissism. All addicts are narcissists.

Affluence continued to increase for the American middle class throughout the 1980s. This decade's generation had no truck with the counterculture movement. They were, however, just as narcissistic as their predecessors. They made no apologies for their unabashed commitment to material well-being. Greed ceased to be a dirty word. As the character portrayed by Michael Douglas in the film *Wall Street* proclaimed, "Greed, for lack of a better word is good. Greed is right. Greed works. Greed clarifies, cuts through and captures the essence of the evolutionary spirit. Greed in all of its forms; greed for life, for money, for love, for knowledge has marked the upward surge of mankind." Greed, most notably, manifests itself in bigger houses and luxury cars. It is also the basis of the need for two incomes for the middle-class family and this, in turn, gives rise to the demand for day-care centers for the children.

Justified by their fulfilling of the American Dream, yuppies substituted a higher standard of living, namely materialism, for quality of family life. As such, they have been exquisite narcissistic role models for their children. They argue that they need two incomes to better provide for their offspring. In actuality, they need dual paychecks to make the payments on the lavish house and expensive cars. With both their parents working, children end up in day care and, when they outgrow the day-care center, become latch-key kids. Unsupervised, their main source of oversight is television. Because the entertainment industry is controlled by narcissists, is it any wonder that the public is bombarded by subject matter that is essentially narcissistic?

It stands to reason that narcissism plays a role in divorce. Love and affection are a sound and indispensable basis for marriage and the creation of families. True love entails more giving than taking. A marriage between two narcissists has three strikes against it from the start because it is a relationship based primarily on taking rather than giving. This understandably spells disaster when the going gets rough since the narcissist demands immediate gratification.

He or she has never learned the value of perseverance and self-sacrifice, a necessary element in the success of any marriage. Divorce has been on a consistent rise since the Civil War. It spiked immediately after World War II then declined during the 1950s although not to the prewar level. Then, at the dawn of the 1960s divorce began to rise exponentially. This phenomenon is not unrelated to the narcissism that began to surface with the '60s generation. It is tempting but nevertheless misleading to think that the increase in the economic independence of women and divorce law reform have played a role in the dramatic rise in divorce. Rather, these are the result of rising expectations of marriage. Rising expectations of marriage implies a lowering of tolerance toward behavior or conditions within marriage. In many ways, this has had an equalizing effect on the partners in a marriage. This is good but it comes with a price. Such equality carries with it the responsibility not to abuse it, which is precisely what happens within marriages between narcissists.

Those narcissists who stay in marriages rather than divorce do no service to their offspring. Such parents make unsatisfactory role models. They only succeed setting their children up to be losers in the game of life by becoming narcissists themselves. Narcissists can never be happy because they can never be satisfied. The narcissist never finds fulfillment because of his constant demand for gratification. More is not enough. There is never enough power or prestige, never too much praise, admiration, never enough material possessions. Consequently, the narcissistic person lives in a constant state of frustration because his needs can never be met.

It is no secret that aggression is an outcome of frustration. This is clearly visible in small children when they "act out." Part of the socializing process, of course, is to teach children to control the natural tendency to be aggressive when frustrated. Ideally, one learns to channel one's aggressiveness in constructive ways. The narcissist never having learned self-control, does not check his aggressiveness which frequently leads to violence. Violence more and more becomes the problem-solving method of choice. There is a direct correlation between narcissism and violent behavior. As we have become a more and more narcissistic society, the more violent we have become. Violence is found not only in the streets and in our schools, it is in our homes as well. Never before has there been so much child abuse and domestic violence. Violence is so widespread throughout our country that we no longer believe that the police can protect us. As a result, the burglar-alarm industry is thriving and the sale of handguns is at an all-time high. These are indicators of a society in decay.

The solution to the problem of violence is not to be found in putting more police on the street. We will survive as a society only if we return to policing ourselves from within. When people behave lawfully only for fear of getting caught, inevitably many of them will think they are clever enough not to get caught and will indiscriminately break the law. When this occurs, chaos results. We can reverse the decay of society by internalizing the concepts of right and wrong and by choosing to reject violence as being inherently evil and to be avoided on that count alone. We need to be proactive in doing what is right simply because it is the right and good thing to do regardless of personal gain or lack thereof. Since every human being is fallible, we must take responsibility for our behavior no matter how unpleasant or difficult that might be. Considering that our values have been under attack since the beginning of the 20th century, it is little wonder that we have become a narcissistic society. We could scarcely avoid it. The question presently confronting us is, "What can we do about it?" Decay of values inescapably leads to the downfall of society. We have two choices. We do nothing and accept our ruination as an inevitability or we commit ourselves to changing our society for the better. For those who desire the latter, the following chapters offer a blueprint for constructive change.

"Selfishness is the greatest curse of the human race."

William Gladstone (1809-1898),
Speech, Hawarden (May 28, 1890)

PART II

CHAPTER TEN

Man, The Moral Creature

With most of the traditional sources of authority having been called into question, it is little wonder why our values have suffered greatly. Without the bulwark of authority how are we to recapture our lost values? One thing is for sure. Values won't be imposed by government decree. Anyone posing as an authority may generate a following. Relatively speaking, however, that following will be a drop in the bucket. The fact of the matter is that external authority in this country has by and large lost its clout. There are two reasons for this. 1) Throughout the entire 20th century almost all manner of external authority, as we have shown, has been systematically undermined. 2) People today are more informed than previous generations. Knowledge in and of itself encourages the independence of people. Authority can no longer just be blindly followed. Armed with knowledge individuals demand justification of authority over their behavior. The mere fact that authority is called upon to justify itself undermines the power of that authority.

Since values gain their strength by virtue of some authority or other, and since the traditional external sources of authority in America have gone by the wayside, what is left? We are left only with ourselves. Each individual must realize that authority may only be found at a personal level. We refer to this as **individual responsibility**. To achieve this involves more than meets the eye.

Step One—MAKING A CHOICE

At the outset, each one of us must consciously choose to take responsibility for our own actions. This takes a great deal of commitment and self-discipline. Unless they consciously choose to do so, individuals will not make the great commitment necessary to empower themselves with authority and, therefore, to take personal responsibility for their own contracts and actions. Taking personal responsibility is the crucial step necessary to reverse the decline of values in this country. Unless a majority of people make the commitment to accept full responsibility for their behavior, the society as we know it will eventually collapse. With such a collapse we lose our freedom and our way of life. Hopefully, most Americans will elect to take personal responsibility once they understand the consequences of not doing so.

Step Two—ACCEPTING OUR MORAL HERITAGE

Human beings, as part of their biology, are endowed with a moral sense, an innate ability to assess certain overt behavior as right or wrong. "The human capacity for a moral motive and its associated emotions took from our primate ancestry a keen sensitivity to the voice, face, and actions of others but added five unique abilities: 1) to infer the thoughts and feelings of others, 2) to be self-aware, 3) to apply the categories good and bad to events and to self, 4) to reflect on past actions and 5) to know that a particular act could have been suppressed. The combination of these five talents created a novel system that first emerges in children in the second year and matures during the decade that follows." (Jerome Kagan, *Three Seductive Ideas*, p. 169).

Two-year-old children express the moral feelings of compassion and justice. At that age, they have had no formal instruction as to the nature of either one of these moral notions. Yet when they are engaged in interactive play where conflicts inevitably occur, one child says to the other, "That's not fair." Fairness, of course, is justice. Both children involved in this type of exchange understand one another. That means that they infer the thoughts and feelings of others; that is, others also possess a moral sense. This is a crucial difference between man and beast.

Compassion among young playmates also has been documented. In one case, two 16 month-old boys were observed fighting over a toy. One boy released the toy when the other started to cry. When the one boy continued to cry, the other boy went to a different room from which he returned with the crying boy's favorite toy. This is a clear sign of compassion. Just and compassionate behaviors have never been successfully documented in other species.

The moral sense is a function of highly conceptual beings. The innate ability of human beings to conceptualize makes interpretation and characterization of overt behavior possible. Take, for example, the killing of one person by another. Killing is simply that, killing. Conceptual creatures, however, demand justification of such overt acts as a function of their moral sense. Justification or evaluation goes beyond the overt act. It is an assessment of it. The killing may be judged to be an act of self-defense or perhaps murder. But those are characterizations of the overt act of killing. Such evaluations inevitably involve the concepts of good and evil.

Our capacity to make moral evaluations is a function of our being conceptual creatures with a moral sense. That we possess a moral sense makes us moral creatures whether we like it or not. Knowing that we are innately moral beings, however, does not mean that we accept that status. The knowledge that we are moral beings entails an understanding that we ought to behave in a moral manner. But there is a huge difference between knowing what the moral thing to do is (in any given situation) and deciding to do it. This stage of empowering oneself with moral authority demands a commitment to doing it; that is, behaving in a moral manner. In other words, in order to really take responsibility for ourselves, we must not only accept our moral sense but embrace it.

Step Three—ENHANCING OUR SELF AWARENESS

A dimension of our ability to conceptualize is being self-aware. Self-awareness makes possible the understanding that evaluations of overt behavior as good or evil apply to oneself as well as others. Additionally, being self-ware allows us to reflect on past actions and to understand that we could have done otherwise. These cognitive realizations have been scientifically verified. They constitute the foundation of the subsequent recognition that we possess free will, that we are the cause of our own actions, that we "own" our behavior. Accepting ownership of our behavior means taking full responsibility for it. Step Three (in the process of self-empowerment) entails understanding that, as innately moral creatures, we possess free will and that we must make a commitment to accepting full responsibility for our behavior. The act of accepting this responsibility is twofold. First of all, we must accept that we are accountable for our deeds. Second, responsibility means that we understand and accept the concept that there are consequences for wrongdoing. Taking full responsibility for our behavior requires that we are willing to admit to wrongdoing and that we accept the necessity to "pay the piper."

Step Four—REJECTING ETHICAL RELATIVISM

The acceptance of ourselves as moral creatures means accepting the existence of good and evil and rejecting ethical relativism. The errors of ethical relativism were discussed in Chapter Three. Understanding the nature of good and evil provides the foundation upon which we can make rational moral choices. In committing ourselves to behaving morally, we empower ourselves with moral authority. Each person so empowered polices his own behavior not because of some external authority or force but because he has willingly accepted the status of the moral creature he innately is.

To truly abandon the idea that values are relative, we must in most respects curb our own narcissistic behaviors. This, first of all, requires that we honestly recognize our own narcissistic tendencies. Second, we must then commit to changing our old patterns of behavior. Such a commitment leads to our controlling our narcissistic ways. And this opens the door to our taking personal responsibility for our behavior.

CHAPTER ELEVEN

Duty

Empowering oneself with moral authority requires taking responsibility for one's behavior. An essential aspect of this is a commitment to fulfilling one's obligations. Obligations often are undertaken through conscious choice. For example, the act of making a promise places the promise-maker under an obligation to fulfill the terms of the promise absent extenuating circumstances. Promises are nothing less than a species of contract.

The making of promises covers a lot of territory. For openers, it means keeping your word. This is a matter of honesty, honesty being a virtue (see Chapter Thirteen). Second, it means not using the excuse of false extenuating circumstances to weasel out of an obligation. This again involves honesty. To avoid misusing extenuating circumstances, we must be brutally honest with ourselves. This a moral duty.

Promises run the gamut from small to very large. Borrowing is an act of promise-making. Borrowing $5 is a small promise. Getting married involves a huge promise. The larger the promise, the greater the obligation one undertakes. Marriage is such a huge act of promise-making because it involves so many unknowns. Even when potentially adverse situations are recognized early on, no one knows what the future will bring. Marriage partners pledge to one another to stick together in sickness and in health, through potential life-altering experiences and with the possibility of changing and growing apart as they experience life's passages. This is a mighty tall order. Yet only four conditions warrant divorce: abuse, adultery, drug addiction, and when children are not involved, a *mutual* agreement to formally dissolve the marriage contract.

The obligations created by marriage are substantially increased by the creation of a family. By creating offspring, parents put themselves under an obligation to raise their kids in a manner by which they grow up to be responsible adults. This entails being good role models for their children. Part and parcel of being a good role model is to honor the promises one makes.

Parents need to reject the model of a "child-centered" home because such an environment robs the child of the values he or she needs to develop into a happy individual successfully integrated into society. The child-centered home cheats the individual of having to learn self-discipline. A child-centered upbringing is dishonest in that it leads the individual to believe he is "special" and, thereby, discourages him from developing perseverance to overcome his weaknesses. Without the quality of perseverance, he cannot be courageous in the face of adversity. In short, child-centered homes produce narcissists. Narcissists lack integrity because they are selfish. Narcissists blame others for their weaknesses and avoid taking responsibility for their own behavior. Narcissists make for irresponsible citizens, unpleasant neighbors, terrible spouses and lousy parents. They make lousy parents because, as the narcissists they are, it is impossible for them to be admirable role models for their offspring. Admirable parental role modeling is absolutely crucial in raising children with values. Children will not grow up to discharge their duties and responsibilities unless they see their parents doing likewise.

A parent's duty is to set a good example for his or her offspring. This includes treating the child with respect so that he will learn to treat others with respect. Respect for people implies a genuine concern for their well-being. It means behaving with civility toward others. Parents cannot teach children honesty unless they behave honestly (and are honest with their kids). Once again, this means being forthright with the children in terms of helping them face their limitations and honesty in evaluating their performance regarding their endeavors. Children see through false praise. They want and deserve honest evaluations of their performance. It is such honesty that lays the foundation for the child developing self-esteem.

An ideal society is one in which everyone possesses a healthy self-concept. True self-esteem is only acquired by honesty, hard work and persistence. Again, it can only be earned, not given. This point is very often overlooked in today's upbringing of children. Many parents and teachers falsely believe that praise, be it earned or not, is sufficient for the development of self-esteem. Kids know better. They want, need and deserve an honest assessment of their behavior and performance. Parents have a duty to give it to them. This concept is at the heart of building true self-esteem in children.

And what goes around comes around. Children tend to parent the way they were parented. If parents don't set good examples for their children, what kind of role models can we expect them to provide when they become parents? Children are not stupid and are very perceptive. What message is being sent to them if one or both parents have affairs? The message is that honesty in general and honesty within the context of marriage is of little value to these parents. It is a message that condones cheating on one's spouse. It is naïve to think that there is no transference of those values from parents to children. To a great extent that is what parenting is all about. The predicament we find ourselves in today is by and large the result of the vicious cycle which is set in motion even when well-intentioned parents raise narcissists who in turn become parents who set a narcissistic example for their own offspring.

Narcissism in one or both partners does not make for a successful marriage. Nevertheless, when two people create another human being, they have an obligation to put the well-being of that child above all else because that child is totally dependent upon them and it had no say in its own creation. Just because the "spark" or excitement has gone out of the relationship is ***absolutely*** no acceptable reason to get divorced. Just because one or both of the parents have grown to dislike the other is ***absolutely*** no acceptable reason to get divorced. Just because one or both of the parents are bored with their spouse is *absolutely* no acceptable reason to get divorced.

Parents obligate themselves when they have children. As the sayings goes, "If you play, you pay." The pay is the awesome responsibility two people create for themselves when bringing another human being into the world. Consequently, if the excitement has gone out of the relationship, they can and are obligated to find a way to spice it up. If they have grown to dislike one another, they can and are obligated to figure out why so that they can start liking one another again. And if parents are bored with each other, they can and are obligated to get un-bored without abusing one another, becoming addicted to drugs or having extramarital affairs. Two people can overcome such difficulties if they fully accept the overriding obligation that goes with creating children. Parents who put their own happiness above the well-being of their children are downright immoral.

This concept applies no less to people who adopt children. Children do not have much chance to fully develop their potential, to develop self-esteem, to take responsibility for their own behavior, to become happy individuals successfully integrated into society unless they have caring parents who provide a loving, honest and stable environment within which a child can grow. Parents who do not strive to provide such an environment for their kids are downright selfish and immoral.

For some, there may appear to be an element of inconsistency in all this. Is not the putting of a child's well-being above all else tantamount to creating a child-centered household? NO. Taking the responsibility to integrate a child into the family and society at large in such a way that the child comes to understand that he is not the center of the universe is the goal. Teaching the child to pursue his innate tendencies of compassion and justice is the goal. Teaching him to be honest with himself and others is the goal.

We cannot conclude this section without addressing the issue of children born out of wedlock. When adults make a choice to have sex, they must take responsibility for that decision. If a child is born of that choice (even if it happens as a result of contraceptive failure), both partners need to realize that this outcome brings with it obligations that must be fulfilled. Part of personal responsibility for adults is the choice of their sexual partners.

We have all heard the mantra: "Be true to yourself." It is used in a variety of contexts. "Be true to yourself" is good counsel when one is agonizing over the choice of a profession or vocation. It is good counsel when prioritizing one's goals. All too frequently, however, "be true to yourself" is used to justify avoiding one's obligations. For a parent to abrogate his obligations to his family for the purpose of "being true" to himself is not an act of honesty. It is an act of cowardice and deceit. It is cowardly because one who uses "being true to yourself" in such a situation demonstrates an unwillingness to face the challenges involved in providing a loving and stable home life. It is deceitful because one has either allowed himself be conned by others to "be true" to himself or has rationalized himself out of his obligations for the sake of "being true" to himself. The bottom line is that the honest meaning of "Being true to yourself" is living up to your commitments whatever they are.

That parental selfishness is pandemic in this society is verified by the proliferation of day-care centers over the past 20 years. There is a constant hue and cry that families cannot "make it" on the salary of one parent, that both parents *need* to work in order to adequately provide for themselves and their children. A scrutiny of the demographics demonstrates that it is a ruse. Most two-income American families do not actually *need* two incomes. The underlying reason for having two incomes is the narcissism of the parents. Here, the affluence of our society has been a major contributing factor. As a nation, we have been enormously successful in creating affluence to the point that affluence is considered to be the be-all and end-all of our existence and so the need for dual incomes.

In the process, quality of life quite frequently has taken a beating. Were it not for the narcissistic desires of the parents to live in a house far larger than the one in which they grew up or the need to drive status automobiles, or to take luxury vacations, there wouldn't be the need for two incomes. In many cases, the cost of clothes for the second breadwinner plus the car expense of getting to and from work plus the cost of day care are barely offset by the second income. Who's kidding whom? More importantly, who is suffering in the process? It is the children stuck in day care who are suffering because their parents are too selfish to realize that fact. Kids deserve better, at least until they start school. They deserve a parent as a fixture of their environment during their formative years. At this stage in their development they do not know, much less care that they are put to bed in a 1500-square-foot house or one twice that size. Children need a parental environment and that should be placed ahead of the desire of the parents to acquire personal possessions.

This does not mean a "child-centered" upbringing. It means a responsible upbringing. It is the job of the parents to provide that upbringing and if they fully accept their parental obligations, they do not ship their kids off to day care. Rather, they delay their own gratification of a larger house, luxurious vacations and fancy cars for the well-being of the person or persons *they* created. Not to do so is fundamentally immoral. Life is about choices. If you don't want the obligations that go along with having kids, then don't have kids. It's really as simple as that. Anyone who casually has a child is irresponsible and immoral period, because it is the child and the children of that child, who inevitably suffer. And since the child has no say in his or her creation such parents create unnecessary suffering, which is immoral (see Chapter Twelve). Every kid deserves to be wanted and loved by his or her parents, not just the baby sitter.

Parental obligations also include being actively involved in the education of one's offspring, both formally and informally. The latter entails providing for the child from day one an environment that encourages learning and the pursuit of satisfying his natural curiosity. "A mind is a terrible thing to waste." Not providing such an environment is a dereliction of parental duty. Regarding formal education, parents are morally obligated to be actively interested and involved in the child's schooling. Make no mistake, it is ultimately the parents' responsibility to educate their children. If a child grows up uneducated, it's not enough to look to the schools. It is the parents' responsibility to monitor this process the whole way. This takes two forms: 1) parents should act in partnership with teachers and school administrators for the purpose of supporting their efforts to educate the child. 2) Parents are obligated to actively oversee the child's homework schedule (not do it for them). This demonstrates to the child the importance parents attach to homework and it fosters self-discipline for the purpose of getting the job done and done well. Taking pride in one's work, as a result of doing it well, is a cornerstone of self-esteem.

Human beings are by nature social creatures. This means that we, as individuals, derive our security from living in groups. This reality carries with it obligations. We, as individuals, have obligations to the group for the purpose of assuring its viability and, therefore, our own individual well-being. Just what are our obligations to the group? Our principal obligation to the group is to try to the best of our ability to avoid evil (see Chapter Twelve). And we also have a duty to behave in a virtuous manner (see Chapter Thirteen).

If individuals have an obligation to society, it follows that society has an obligation to the individuals who comprise that society. This area of obligation has everything to do with the culture wars that we are presently experiencing in this country. Such are deemed social problems. For example, single-parent households constitute an enormous problem in this country. These are the result of both accidental and intentional pregnancies. Many accidental pregnancies are brought to term because one or both of the parents reject abortion. Abortion is a centerpiece of our culture wars. Notwithstanding the irresponsibility of the parents in accidentally creating the child, the child is a reality and society has an obligation to protect that child from neglect and abuse. The degree to which society is responsible for and to the unwanted child is also a function of cultural warfare. One thing is for sure. Society is obligated to track down deadbeat fathers and mothers, whether they are partners in a wanted or unwanted child. Society at large is morally obligated to go to whatever extremes are necessary to force deadbeat fathers and mothers to monetarily support their offspring.

Intentional pregnancies are an altogether different issue. We have seen a steady increase in the number of women who have chosen to create a child with no intention of marrying or settling down with its father. This is immoral because is the epitome of selfishness. This selfishness typically takes two forms. 1) "I don't want to share the kid with someone else." 2) "I can't seem to find an adequate partner to share the responsibility of parenthood who also loves ME. Nevertheless, I can't be true to **MYSELF** unless I have a child." This is narcissism to the max. How sad for the child to have a consummate narcissist as a role model regardless of what economic advantages the child might have. To consciously raise a child in such an environment is, again, downright immoral.

On the other hand, another phenomenon occurring in society is that of single adults adopting children. Women or men, for that matter, adopting a child even without the intention of marrying, is not only moral but praiseworthy. Since all children deserve to be wanted and loved, single people adopting children should be praised. Most certainly, no one has a moral obligation to adopt children. To do so, however, is clearly virtuous. It is an expression of the non-moral virtue of courage, an act above and beyond the call of duty.

Another area where the society at large has obligations pertains to poverty. It is most perplexing that the most affluent country in the world is riddled with pockets of poverty. According to the rhetoric heard from many of our politicians, the elimination of poverty is a national priority. If this were true poverty would have been eradicated long ago. So why do we as a society tolerate poverty? The answer is to be found in the values upon which this society was founded, namely the Protestant work ethic and the U.S. constitution that guarantees individuals a "right to the pursuit of happiness", not a right to happiness itself. The former is the view that working and working hard is good. The latter maintains that success is a function of individual perseverance and if one is disadvantaged it is not only possible but also incumbent upon that individual to pull *himself* up by his bootstraps. With these values dictating the societal mindset, is it any wonder why poverty is tolerated?

The poverty problem transcends race, although it would be disingenuous to suggest that racism plays no role in it. Poverty is allowed to exist because the underlying values of American society dictate that each individual be ultimately responsible for himself. Economic disadvantage is no excuse to drop out along the path to success. Race is irrelevant to success. Any individual can "make it" if he is willing to sacrifice and persevere. And to belabor this argument, there is no shortage of individual success stories. The fact remains, however, that the individuals of such success stories are exceptions to the rule. To a great extent, the decline of the inner city has occurred as a result of government programs that almost encourage poverty and the positions of many ethnic leaders who promote anything but a move to personal responsibility.

The root causes of poverty, strictly speaking, are not due to culture wars. They run far deeper than our present culture wars. This country will not be able to adequately deal with this problem of poverty until it honestly confronts its fundamental mindset concerning it. This is a most difficult task since that mindset to a great extent defines us as Americans.

CHAPTER TWELVE

Evil

In Chapter Ten, we addressed the fact that human beings are uniquely moral creatures. As such we have an obligation to do our level best to avoid evil. In order to effectively turn away from evil, we must first know what evil is. Evil, in most respects, is another word for pain and all normal creatures capable of sensation by nature attempt to avoid pain. So evil is rooted in fact, a fact being defined as the way things actually are in the world. Consequently, there is nothing relative about facts and because evil is rooted in fact, there is nothing relative about evil either. It is very important to understand the objective nature of evil because it then follows that what is evil is evil for you, me or anyone else as well; what counts as evil is not a matter of opinion as some would like to argue.

Pain is understood to be evil because it is the chief indicator of harm. However, not all pain is harmful. Some pain is necessary because it leads to some good. Going to a dentist may be painful. Nevertheless, one suffers the experience with the expectation that the resulting good will offset the present pain and prevent the increased harm and future pain that would ensue by not seeing the dentist in the first place. In such cases, we say that such pain is instrumental to some future good, or simply that it is instrumentally good. So some pain is judged to be necessary and therefore instrumentally good. Furthermore, some of the pain resulting from our actions may be unintentional. With the exceptions of unintentional pain and instrumental pain, all other pain is evil.

Since a person is morally obligated to avoid evil, it follows that he is morally obligated to avoid causing intentional or unnecessary pain to any creature capable of sensation. Any creature that feels pain is a player in the moral scheme of things. And although animals are not moral creatures themselves, they most certainly are the objects of much human behavior. That is why cruelty to animals is morally corrupt. Such cruelty has nothing to do with animal rights. Animal rights are a myth. Crushing a dog's foot for the fun of it is morally depraved simply because it hurts the dog, not because the dog has an inherent right to be free from abuse.

As human beings, we have the ability to extrapolate upon our painful experiences. Such extrapolation involves (a) understanding that such experiences are evil and should be avoided, (b) that there exist other creatures capable of sensation, and (c) since we know that we can choose how we behave, we should avoid choosing to do evil. In other words, we should avoid that which we judge will cause intentional or unnecessary pain for other sentient beings. What we do and how we behave is a matter of choice. Therefore, the element of judgment plays a key role in moral decision-making. That one individual judges an action to be necessary yet painful and another person judges the same action to be unnecessary does not legitimize ethical relativism. For example, it has been and still is customary in certain African countries to engage in the practice of female genital mutilation. When a girl becomes of age, her clitoris and frequently her labia are crudely and non-hygienically cut off without the aid of anesthesia. That these African cultures judge this procedure to be necessary although painful does not mean that female genital mutilation is **in fact** necessary. Differences in judgment about the facts simply means that those involved in the judging process cannot both be right. The action in question either leads to unnecessary pain or it does not. When one judges an action to be necessary yet painful when **in fact** it is unnecessary, that judgment is mistaken. When we act on mistaken judgments we can say that, from a moral point of view, we have failed. We may have acted with good intentions but as the saying goes, "The road to hell is paved with good intentions." To be a moral person requires more than good intentions. It means acting in a moral manner as a result of correct moral decision-making.

The most primitive sort of pain is physical. But human beings are more than physical creatures; we are also self-aware. Without self-awareness, a human being has no basis by which to recognize himself as a moral being. This is what differentiates the moral sense from our other five senses. The moral sense is a function of higher-level consciousness whereas the other five senses are physically oriented. Higher-level consciousness makes it possible for us to experience psychological pain. Feeling betrayed is an example of psychological pain. So evil pertains to actions that cause either intentional or unnecessary physical or psychological pain for a sentient being.

Let us suppose that someone who is single is contemplating having an affair with a married person. Suppose further that this would-be adulterer is most clever and calculates that he and his would-be partner can get away with the deed without ever being found out. This person could reason that since the affair would not cause pain to anyone, it would not be an evil thing to do. And since it would not be an evil thing to do, it would be morally all right to proceed with the affair. According to what has so far been determined to be evil, namely pain, our adulterer seemingly would be correct. However, since no one can be 100 percent sure of the future, there is always the possibility that our adulterers will be caught and this will result in someone's pain. Since affairs always have the potential to cause pain, therefore, they ought to be avoided.

This line of reasoning applies primarily to the single person involved in the affair. So far as the married partner is concerned, the initiation of an affair should have been rejected on the grounds that married people have a duty to avoid such behavior because by getting married, the partners have promised each other that they would be faithful to one another and thus avoid affairs.

One will not be successful at making moral decisions if these decisions are made in a haphazard manner. Success is a result of consistency. By making decisions based on a moral principle and always on the same principle, one achieves moral consistency. Having determined what is evil, the moral principle that is the standard by which we ought to make moral decisions can be formulated. Since as moral creatures we have a moral obligation to avoid evil, *one ought not choose to do that which he honestly believes can cause actual or potential intentional or unnecessary physical or psychological pain for any sentient being.*

People are confronted with choices every day. Some of these choices are moral ones. It is naive to think that they can be avoided. In Chapter Ten, we saw that to be human is to know that we have free will, which means that any given action could have been suppressed. Sometimes, out of frustration, people "act out." If such "acting out" takes the form of kicking the dog or abusing one's spouse or kids, such behavior is immoral. First of all, an adult has the choice not to vent his frustration in such a manner. Second, behaving in such a way causes actual unnecessary pain for a sentient being. That's why such behavior is immoral.

Some moral choices are simple ones such as the choice to kick the dog or not kick the dog. One alterative is evil, the other alternative is not evil. The choice of whether or not to do the act is simple because it doesn't present a genuine dilemma. However, we are quite frequently confronted with a genuine moral dilemma, a situation in which we must choose between two equally unattractive moral courses of action. For example, suppose that the life of a very close relative is dependent upon his having an operation. The surgeon confides in you that it will be extremely and unavoidably painful. He is evasive about the subject in the presence of your relative because he knows as do you that if this relative has a clue as to the amount of pain involved he may well decide to forego the operation and therefore most likely would die. Your relative pleads with you to tell him the truth. What ought you do: tell the truth or lie? There is no way off the hook here and that is why it is a genuine moral dilemma. The only consistent way to extract oneself from a moral dilemma is by reliance on a moral principle and always on the same moral principle. To do otherwise is to court evil which one has a moral obligation to avoid. Reliance on a moral principle doesn't necessarily make the decision easier. What it does do is provide the reassurance that, over the long haul, one will be morally successful.

Some people may attempt to get off the hook of making moral decisions in accordance with a moral principle by arguing that one can never be 100 percent sure of the outcome of their actions. Since the outcome of our actions is never a sure thing, we may as well not worry about it and make moral decisions as the moment dictates. Such a view of moral decision-making is irresponsible. It is a fact that consistency in decision-making always leads to better results than inconsistency. Even though it is true that we can never be 100 percent sure of the outcome of our actions, one thing is for sure. By consistently using the same moral principle to guide our moral decisions, we will achieve a higher degree of success in being a moral person than by not doing so. Therefore, if one commits himself to being as moral a person as possible, then he is obligated to consistently use the same moral principle to make his moral decisions.

Unfortunate as it may be, moral decision-making frequently is unforgiving. Many of the moral dilemmas we face are excruciatingly difficult. Nevertheless, the refusal to deal with such difficulty is a choice in itself and is a morally irresponsible one. It is by accepting our status as moral beings, making decisions in accordance with the above stated moral principle and fully accepting the consequences of them that one becomes a bona fide moral agent.

The turning away from evil and becoming a moral agent will bring great rewards to both you and the people that are touched by your life. It will increase your self worth. It will assist in growing the self worth of your children. And finally, actualizing your moral agency will help others do so as well.

CHAPTER THIRTEEN

Virtue

Values and virtues to a great extent go hand-in-hand. Virtue refers to behavior that is admired or considered praiseworthy. An individual is not considered virtuous, however, on the basis of one or two commendable acts. Rather, virtue is a disposition. Dispositions are either instinctive or acquired tendencies to behave in one way or another. Of course, not all dispositions are admired, for as we all know, some people have lousy dispositions. Those dispositions that we admire are understood to be virtuous. This dispositional nature of virtue leads people to think of virtues as character traits. It should come as no surprise that virtuous behavior embodies what people value. Values and virtues to a great extent go hand-in-hand.

Many people mistakenly believe that all virtues possess a moral dimension. However, some virtues are moral and some are not. Moral virtues are ones that a person has a duty to perform; non-moral virtues are those a person is not duty bound to perform but are virtues that are above and beyond the call of duty.

Moral Virtues

Justice and compassion are moral virtues but they are unique among virtues because they are instinctive dispositions. All other virtues require training and practice. In Chapter Ten, we made reference to the moral sense possessed uniquely by human beings. It is this moral sense that makes us moral creatures unlike the rest of the animal kingdom. In addition to the physical senses, we are born with a moral sense. We by nature recognize situations as fair or unfair and are naturally disposed to treat others fairly. Justice is fairness. Similarly, we are instinctively compassionate concerning the plight of people other than ourselves. We empathize with them because deep down we realize that we could suffer the same plight. In a very real sense, we understand that "there but for the grace of God go I."

Though individuals come by justice and compassion instinctively, these feelings need to be nurtured by a favorable environment to become fully developed. Negative external influences such as bigotry and hate can effectively stunt the development of these feelings. Since children have no control over the environment in which they are raised, it is incumbent upon their parents to provide them with an environment that enhances the virtues characteristic of the moral sense.

Responsibility is a moral virtue. The notion "to be responsible" is ambiguous. On the one hand, a person is responsible *for* what he did; that is, he was the author or cause of, say setting the fire that destroyed the barn. Alternatively, a person is responsible *to* someone; that someone may be a person, group or an authority to which he is accountable. As the causal agent of the arson, the fire starter is held responsible *for* the action and he is responsible *to* society, because he should not have done what he did. Society will hold the arsonist accountable for his behavior since he was the author (cause) of it.

It is an altogether different issue, however, for the arsonist to take responsibility for his actions. For him to be a moral agent, he must accept responsibility for his behavior. Virtue lies on the side of one holding himself accountable for his misdeeds and a willingness to pay the price. Admittedly, this is an extreme example. It was chosen to demonstrate the causal factor that is an essential aspect of responsibility. We all have on occasion freely chosen to do something immoral either by not fulfilling some obligation or by intentionally harming someone. The issue at stake here is how we deal with our misdeeds. Purely and simply, we have a duty to willingly take responsibility for them and accept whatever punishment is imposed.

As we have already seen in the previous chapter on duty, we create many of our obligations by our own choosing. Such obligations are the result of some sort of contract such as making a promise that we freely enter into. **Honesty** compels us to keep our promises. Honesty, however, is, much more than keeping the promises we make. To lie, cheat and steal is to be dishonest. All forms of honesty and its opposite dishonesty affect other human beings either for good or bad. That is why honesty is a moral virtue and because it is a moral virtue, we are duty bound to do our level best to be honest in our various and sundry dealings with other people. When we are honest and accept full responsibility for our behavior, we are judged as having integrity.

We are social creatures, which is to say that our survival depends on the survival of others. Consequently, we should be concerned about the well-being and well-fare of others. Such concern, however, should extend beyond an interest in our own survival. All human beings as moral creatures are deserving of a mutual respect for one another. We cannot have a genuine concern for our fellow human beings unless we possesses an underlying respect for them. **Concern for others** is a moral virtue dependent upon **respect for others**, which is also a moral virtue. While not virtues themselves, civility and decency are ways of demonstrating respect for other people and because of that fact they are valued.

Selfishness competes with a concern for others. Selfishness is trying to gain something at the expense of others. The opposite of selfishness is unselfishness. Therefore, **unselfishness** is a moral virtue. It is unselfishness that provides a basis for our concern for others. This can be understood by noting that quite frequently demonstrating a concern for others requires some sacrifice on our part. A selfish person simply won't make such sacrifices. Truly selfish persons couldn't care less about the well-being much less the well-fare of other individuals. Selfishness is a characteristic of narcissism. Narcissists are self-centered. Consequently, they do not discharge their duties nor do they take responsibility for their behavior. They lack courage, self-discipline and perseverance. Bluntly speaking, they lack virtue because they are the epitome of selfishness.

Justice, compassion, responsibility, honesty, concern and respect for others and unselfishness are moral virtues. We have a duty to incorporate such virtues into our behavior because other people are adversely affected when we do not. No man is an island. Each and every one of us is a member of the human community. As members of that community, therefore, we have a duty to incline our behavior accordingly.

It is the duty of all parents to instill good habits of virtuous behavior in their offspring. Habits are learned behaviors. Children learn best by example. Therefore, one of the primary duties of parents is to set good examples of virtuous behavior for their children so that they too may learn these habits. Children are far more perceptive than many people realize. They see through deceit and phoniness. Parents who raise their children under the do-as-I-say-and-not-as-I-do principle are simply irresponsible. Parents who direct their children to tell the truth then lie themselves send a double message. If parents do not live virtuously, chances are neither will their children.

Furthermore, parents are duty-bound to discipline their offspring. The purpose of discipline is to set limits on behavior for without such limits, parents cannot successfully teach their children the difference between right and wrong, good and evil. Additionally, a disciplined environment is a perquisite for the development of virtues. Discipline does not come naturally. Remember, an undisciplined "child-centered" upbringing produces a narcissist. And as we have seen, narcissists are themselves undisciplined and egocentric. Narcissists are incapable of virtuous behavior.

Nonmoral Virtues

Self-discipline is the virtue of setting limits on oneself. Since deep down we all have narcissistic tendencies, self-discipline does not come naturally. We develop self-discipline by internalizing the discipline imposed on us by our parents or other authority figures. Self-discipline is of utmost importance because success at any endeavor cannot be achieved without it.

Perseverance or **persistence** is a virtue that is dependent upon self-discipline. Refusing to give up in the face of adversity takes self-discipline. To force oneself to complete the task at hand, unpleasant or not, takes self-discipline. We need perseverance to achieve our goals over time. Goals of great value are not achieved easily. It requires extended hard work. Take, for example, the perseverance necessary to become an Olympic contender, a medical doctor, a skilled craftsman or an astronaut. Those who become successful at these and at many other endeavors do so only through persistence. Perseverance is the key to success at achieving any long sought-after goal.

Both self-discipline and perseverance are nonmoral virtues. Strictly speaking, we are not morally obligated to maintain these character traits. Maintaining them, of course, presupposes that we have them in the first place. Here, the point is that parents have a moral obligation to instill in their offspring the virtues of self-discipline and perseverance. Even though parents have fulfilled their obligation and instilled those virtues in their offspring, the offspring have no moral obligation to be self-disciplined or to persevere. There is the presumption that once virtues are instilled, the habit of behaving virtuously will prevail, but this is only a presumption. As we all know, habits can be changed both for the good and for the bad. So it is not only possible but also plausible that someone can consciously choose not to be self-disciplined or not to persevere and thereby sacrifice long-range goals. Of course, the consequence of not maintaining these virtues typically is failure in life's pursuits. However, no one is **morally** obligated to be self-disciplined or to have long-range goals.

Another non-moral virtue is **charity**. We are not morally obligated to engage in acts of charity. Nevertheless, such behavior is admired. We have no moral obligation to give to the United Way or the Salvation Army. That these organizations clearly do good works is indisputable. But from a moral point of view such good works are beside the point. We are morally obligated only to do our duty and to avoid acting in an evil way. Charitable acts do not qualify. They are above and beyond the call of duty.

Charity poses a problem because there are no defined limits to it. If we are morally obligated to be charitable, then to what extent are we so obligated? Are we obligated to give to charity 10 percent of our net worth? Half of what we own? The shirts off our backs? This brings into focus the idea that to be a virtuous person means more than being a moral person. A moral person is one who fulfills his obligations and earnestly attempts to avoid evil. Such a person is not necessarily a completely virtuous individual because one will be moral even if he chooses not to engage in non-moral virtuous acts.

Next on the list of nonmoral virtues is **patriotism**, the love for or devotion to country. A patriot loves his country and defends and promotes its interests and supports the policies of the national government. We do not have a moral obligation to be patriotic although we most certainly have an obligation to obey the laws of the land where we choose to live. No government is morally pure. Every government is made up of people and it is our responsibility as citizens to hold government officials accountable and responsible for upholding the ideals upon which our country was founded. If those government representatives do not live up to such ideals, then the citizenry has absolutely no responsibility to support them. Genuine patriotism is not a one-way street, a matter of "my Country, right or wrong," If anything, such a view of patriotism is socially irresponsible. In fact, the whole statement proclaimed by Carl Schurz is, "Our country right or wrong. When right, to be kept right; when wrong, to be put right." Patriotism is properly a function of legitimate government representation holding to the ideals upon which that government was founded.

Courage is another non-moral virtue. It is the strength of character that allows us to take calculated risks in life. Taking calculated risks requires knowing what the risks are. In short, it presupposes knowledge of a situation and knowledge of one's abilities relative to that situation. Courageous behavior is strictly a rational affair. Taking calculated risks does not mean that the courageous person will not experience hardship. Rather the hardship is weighed against the value of the goal to be achieved. If the goal is impossible, such hardship is for naught, which is foolish. Those who joined the Freedom Rides in 1961 exhibited a classic example of courageous behavior. The Congress of Racial Equality sponsored the rides from Washington, D.C., into the South as an act of protest against segregated buses and terminals. Seven blacks and six white volunteers were on board two buses. When they reached Alabama, hostile locals stormed the buses, dragged the riders out and beat them with pipes, key rings and fists. The Freedom Riders suffered greatly at the hands of these angry mobs. However, they also knew that there would be national television coverage of their ordeal. The calculated risk was that whatever pain and suffering they experienced, the nation at large would be sufficiently outraged that the Supreme Court ruling that rendered segregated buses and terminals in interstate travel unconstitutional finally would be enforced. The unmasking of evil, publicly exposing the evil behavior of others, requires courage. The reason that this is presently considered illegitimate is because of the widespread acceptance of ethical relativism. Remember, this is the belief that one person's ideas concerning good and evil are just as legitimate as anyone else's. If good and evil are either a matter of personal preference or determined by a given subculture, sitting in judgment of another's behavior will seem arrogant and uncalled for. As has been demonstrated, however, ethical relativism is unfounded and ought to be rejected.

One sure way of reducing the evil that men do is by exposing it. One can take the high road in this regard only if he has empowered himself with moral authority. Otherwise, the public exposure of evil simply reduces to name calling. Accepting full responsibility for our own behavior is not enough to save this society from moral collapse. We must hold those who choose to abrogate their moral authority accountable for their behavior since such abrogation means that they have chosen not to take responsibility for it.

Courage takes guts. Taking a moral stand is not always a popular thing to do. But that is no excuse not to be courageous and take that moral stand and be courageous. One example of widespread cowardice took place during the early 1950s when our civil liberties came under attack and many failed to stand up to Senator Joseph McCarthy and his witch hunt for communists in government and the entertainment industry. Those few who did speak out against this obscenity paid a heavy price. They would not have been forced to pay so dearly if a greater number of citizens had taken a stand against Red baiting.

Alternatively, we saw what can happen when great numbers of people are courageous and challenge government policy. Few people today believe that our involvement in Vietnam during the 1960s was either prudent or moral. Yet, it was because individuals, one by one, had the courage to stand up and publicly criticize our government for being there that our government finally extricated itself. That took guts. It certainly was not a very popular thing to do at first. But again, taking a moral stand frequently involves paying a price.

Nevertheless, no one has a moral obligation to be courageous. To be courageous is acting above and beyond the call of duty. Those who went on the Freedom rides were not **morally** obligated to do so. What they did went beyond the call of duty. We are morally obligated only to do our duty, avoid evil and be morally virtuous.

To live a virtuous life is not always easy or pleasant. Good habits make virtuous behavior easier than not having good habits at all. As for pleasure, doing one's duty or behaving virtuously is not always the most pleasant alternative but that is the price we pay for empowering ourselves with moral authority. Alternatively, a thoroughly narcissistic person is a slave to pleasure. Pleasure guides his behavior to the detriment of himself, those around him and society at large.

CHAPTER FOURTEEN

Authenticity, Self-Esteem and Happiness

As we saw in Chapter Ten, human beings are uniquely moral creatures. That is, unlike any other species of animal, we are born with a moral sense. This is an indisputable fact. As we saw in the previous chapter, however, that moral sense can be stunted. In order for a moral sense to fully develop, children need to grow up in an environment that is conducive to such development. Such an environment should to be one in which we are taught that we have a duty to the human community to behave in a morally virtuous manner. We are duty-bound to fulfill the obligations we voluntarily create for ourselves and we are obligated to avoid evil to the best of our ability. Providing this moral learning environment is the primary duty of parents. They cannot effectively provide it unless they themselves practice what they preach. If parents are successful in this awesome task of responsibly raising children, chances are that their offspring will as a matter of habit and conditioning function as moral agents. Ideally, as moral creatures, they will choose to live in a moral way because they understand that they *ought* to behave in such a manner. These offspring then have the moral foundation to become successful at raising their own children.

The harsh reality though is that the environments in which our children have been raised have to a great extent degenerated from a moral point of view as well as in the teaching of non-moral values. Parents have abrogated their fundamental duties as parents by not providing the necessary environments by which their offspring are trained in values and morals. The primary reason for this breakdown is that these parents were themselves insufficiently trained in values and morals.

We have also seen a vicious cycle developing that can be traced back to the beginning of the 20th century, at which point we as a nation began to head down the path of devaluation and the sabotage of morals. If we continue down this path, the result will be moral anarchy, a state of no morality at all. When this occurs, all that is left is survival of the fittest and general lawlessness. Such a state is ripe for dictatorship. There is an abundance of historical evidence to justify such a prediction. Our freedom literally depends upon our resurrecting the values and morals that made our greatness as a nation possible.

The decline in values and morals is a result of the authority of family, schools, government and church having been challenged over the course of the 20th century. I have argued that to rectify this state of affairs, we must consciously choose to empower ourselves with moral authority. We do this first by **recognizing** and then by **accepting** the fact that we are moral creatures. Fully accepting ourselves as moral creatures means that we understand that we possess free will and that we commit ourselves to accepting full responsibility for our behavior. A moral person also strives to do his duty by fulfilling his obligations, which includes behaving in a morally virtuous manner. And a moral person earnestly tries to avoid evil, namely by not harming other sentient beings. In so doing, a person empowers himself with moral authority. By empowering ourselves with moral authority, we actualize our nature which is that of a moral being. By actualizing our essence, namely that of a moral human being, we can become authentic individuals. An authentic individual is one who is genuine and credible.

Self-esteem is a function of authenticity. It is through authenticity that we earn self-esteem. Once again, self-esteem cannot be given. It must be earned. Being a moral person is not the easiest thing on earth because we all have narcissistic tendencies. Often, we would really rather not do that which we know to be moral. It is not uncommon that we face a conflict between what we want to do and what we know we ought do. To win such battles requires self-discipline and quite frequently a great deal of it. The payoff to winning these moral battles is the satisfaction of knowing that you've done the right thing, that you have actualized yourself as the moral being you are, and that makes you an authentic person. Not all moral situations give rise to conflict. Many times we do the moral thing straightaway. The better our moral habits, the fewer the conflicts. So becoming a moral person requires self-discipline and good habits. The ultimate in self-esteem is to know that we are authentic, that we are living up to what we as humans uniquely are.

Being a moral person also requires that one be honest with oneself. Rationalizing our immoral behavior is an act of being dishonest with ourselves. Such rationalizing takes several forms.

1) Justifying immoral actions on the grounds that others do it is simply unacceptable. Morality is a characteristic of actions themselves, not a matter of who does or does not engage in such behavior. If that were the case, then murdering someone would be morally acceptable *because* other people do it. And that is absurd.

2) Twisting the Golden Rule to one's advantage will not do either. "Do unto others as you would have them do unto you" is easily misinterpreted as "If someone else were in my shoes would it be okay for him to do what I am contemplating doing." The problem with this interpretation is that no one else, strictly speaking, can be in your shoes or they would *be* you. Since no one else qualifies to be in your shoes, you are free and clear to do whatever you please, be it moral or otherwise. Obviously, this is contrary to the intent of the Golden Rule.

3) "Being true to myself" is another way of rationalizing one's behavior. Unless we are scrupulously honest with ourselves, this is simply a way of justifying what we want to do regardless of the moral implications of so doing.

4) Justifying an immoral action on the basis that it really won't make any difference constitutes moral indifference. It is an

outright admittance to wrongdoing covered by a thin veneer of sidestepping the issue. Quite often, petty theft is justified on this basis. "After all, the business from which I am stealing can easily absorb the loss and most likely will never be the wiser." Such a justification avoids the fact that petty theft is nevertheless theft and thieving is immoral.

Watch out for the above traps. If you are truly set on actualizing your authenticity as a moral human being, you should be aware of the traps along the way. Even without these traps, it is a rough road.

Finally, it is safe to say that no one can be truly happy unless he possesses self-esteem. People lack self-esteem because either consciously or unconsciously they know they lack authenticity. This makes perfect sense. If at some level a person knows that he is not authentic, he knows that he is a phony. He knows that he is a disingenuous person. He may not be able to articulate to himself his phoniness because it is rooted in his subconscious self. Nevertheless, there is a feeling there, a persistent uneasy feeling that he can't put his finger on. This situation frequently leads one down the garden path of substituting fame and/or wealth for authenticity.

Fame and/or wealth are commonly thought to be a means to happiness. There are, however, all too many examples that that is simply not the case. More often than not, famous and/or wealthy people are anything but happy. The reason so many people falsely believe that fame and/or wealth are the means to a happy life is because fame and/or wealth appeal to the inherent narcissism of people. The only solution to this rather sad state of affairs is for people to realize that happiness is a product of self-esteem and self-esteem is a product of authenticity. One only becomes authentic by actualizing the moral side of his being. Historically, people have been aided in this actualizing process by religion.

Absent some external authority such as God to motivate one to commit to being a moral person, one must empower himself with moral authority. This, as has been discussed, takes an enormous amount of self-discipline. But the payoff is greatly rewarding, the knowledge that difficult as it may have been, one has succeeded in becoming a moral person. Such is true happiness. One simply cannot be truly happy unless he commits himself to being as moral a person as possible. And if enough individuals commit themselves to being as moral as possible, the moral fiber of this country can be restored.

There is no time like the present to change. You can only change yourself. You will find that, as you make an ongoing commitment to the principle of taking responsibility for your own behavior, others will see the change in you and will follow your example. It is with the acceptance of individual responsibility, done person by person, that our country will be put right and our lost values will return.

BIBLIOGRAPHY

Anderson, Terry, *The Sixties* (N.Y.: Longman, 1999).

Bloom, Lynn Z., *Doctor Spock: Biography of a Conservative Radical* (Indianapolis/N.Y.: The Bobbs-Merrill Co., Inc., 1972).

Cremin, Lawrence A., *The Transformation of the School* (N.Y.: Vintage Books, 1961).

Dewey, John, *The School and Society* (Chicago: The University of Chicago Press, 1900).

_____, *Democracy and Education* (N.Y.: The Free Press, 1966).

Herskovits, Melville J., *Cultural Relativism* (N.Y.: Vintage Books, 1973).

Holt, Luther, *The Care and Feeding of Children: A Catechism for the Use of Mothers and Children's Nurses* (N.Y.: D. Appleton & Co., 1918).

Huber, Peter W., *Liability* (N.Y.: Basic Books, Inc., 1988).

Medved, Michael, *Hollywood vs. America* (N.Y.: Harper Perennial, 1993).

Miller, Douglas T. and Novak, Marion, *The Fifties* (Garden City, N.Y.: Doubleday & Co., Inc., 1975).

Phillips, Roderick, *Untying the Knot* (Cambridge: Cambridge University Press, 1991).

Sykes, Charles J., *A Nation of Victims: The Decay of the American Character* (N.Y.: St. Martins Press, 1992).

Spock, Benjamin, *The Common Sense Book of Baby and Child Care* (N.Y.: Duell, Sloan and Pearce, 1946).

Stern, Aaron, *Me: The Narcissistic American* (N.Y.: Ballantine Books, 1979).

Stevenson, Charles L., *Ethics and Language* (New Haven: Yale University Press, 1944).